D1799634

Spin Bowling

SPORTING SKILLS SERIES

Spin Bowling

RAY ILLINGWORTH

WITH THE ASSISTANCE OF RALPH ELLIS
OF REG HAYTER LTD

PELHAM BOOKS

First published in Great Britain by
PELHAM BOOKS LTD
52 Bedford Square
London WC1B 3EF
1979

Photographs by Patrick Eagar

ISBN 0 7207 1144 4

Photoset in Great Britain by Granada Graphics,
printed by Hollen Street Press, Slough and
bound by Dorstel Press, Harlow

Contents

Introduction

A good spinner is a match winner. On his day he is virtually unplayable, making the ball leap, turn and fly to deceive a procession of helpless victims – you only have to watch Derek Underwood at work on a turning wicket to know that. And when things are not in his favour the spinner is still vital for his ability to bowl a succession of tight, containing overs without a break. To do that you need nagging accuracy, bags of confidence, and a few different deliveries to keep the batsman guessing all the time.

That is a tall order, but the great thing about spin bowling is that it is an art which can be learnt. In that sense it is different from fast bowling. A fast bowler either has the natural ability to hurl the ball down quickly, or he hasn't. And if he can't do it then there is no way you can coach it into him. The reverse is true of spin bowling. I believe that you can learn it from scratch, regardless of your natural size and aptitudes. And that is what I want to help with in this book.

I'll assume you have already learnt the basic grips – and suffered the confusing theories that too many coaching manuals, and coaches, have to offer. So what I am going to concentrate on are the qualities that can turn you from an average slow bowler into a really good spinner. Believe me, there's a crucial difference.

Spin bowling is very much a battle of wits. You haven't got the power that a pace bowler has, so you have to do something with the ball to deceive the batsman into thinking it is easy. If a fast bowler gets hit for four, then he can thunder in, all aggression, and try to pin the batsman to the sightscreen. The spinner can't do that. He has to stay cool, and keep working at it, trying to commit the batsman to a mistake.

To be able to do that you must never stop *thinking*. Concentration is vital. And this is one of the reasons why, however much promise you show, you won't become a good spinner overnight. It is a thinker's game, and the older you get the more successfully you learn to think someone out. I was twenty-six when I played my first Test match, and it took me years after that to become England's regular off-spinner. I was forty-six when I retired from playing – and I still think that if someone gave me a new back and two fresh legs I would be a better bowler in another five years than I was when I was at my peak.

You never stop learning in cricket. Over the years I have watched other bowlers – and I have picked up a few things by watching batsmen too. Now I can look at how they hold the bat, their stance, and how they use their feet, and it tells me a lot about how I am going to bowl to them. I'll let you into the secrets of that later.

What I am trying to explain is why a good spinner is so exciting to watch, and so difficult to bat against. He uses surprise as a weapon, pushing in a quicker ball, tossing up a slower one, always trying to make the batsman play a rash stroke.

I loved bowling to someone like Barry Richards. He accepts the challenge you offer him, and looks for runs – and you know that if you keep attacking he'll try to hit you through the covers once too often. It is a battle of wits. You are after him, he is after you, like duelling swordsmen, attacking and defending, and looking for an opening to strike each other out of the game. Crowds love it. It's a contest, it's entertainment. It's what cricket is all about.

It saddens me that the modern one-day game has made it so difficult for a spinner to come through. I often wonder if I would have been so successful if I were starting my career again now, having to bowl in so many different competitions. Once a spinner has learnt his craft then he can do as much as anyone to keep the run rate down, and can play an invaluable role in limited-overs cricket. I took four wickets for only five runs in a John Player League match against Worcestershire in 1972 on a day when the seamers barely took a wicket between them. Of course that was a turning wicket, and I had already learnt how to peg a batsman down. For a young, inexperienced bowler on a good wicket, things aren't so easy.

Often John Player League games are played on smaller grounds with short boundaries, which makes it easy for a batsman to ruin a young bowler's confidence with a string of fours and sixes. That makes it very difficult to give a youngster a long spell of bowling. But I would love to see the rules altered to *make* counties bowl spinners, and help their young players to gain experience. For example, one or two bowlers on each side could be permitted an unrestricted run-up, whereas the rest would be limited to within, say, six yards. That way the really quick bowlers could go flat out – and teams would have to use genuine spinners the remainder of the time. That would put a stop to the continual medium-pace attack which so many teams use in one-day games, and which is in danger of creeping into County Championship matches.

Fast bowlers and good spinners are the greatest things in cricket. They are the people crowds love to watch, because they make things happen. If you still doubt that a spinner can be effective in a limited-overs match, then think back to the 1978 Gillette Cup final at Lord's. Somerset's Viv Richards, arguably the world's best batsman, had made a dashing start against the seamers. But the Sussex slow left-armer Giles Cheatle pegged him down to just a few

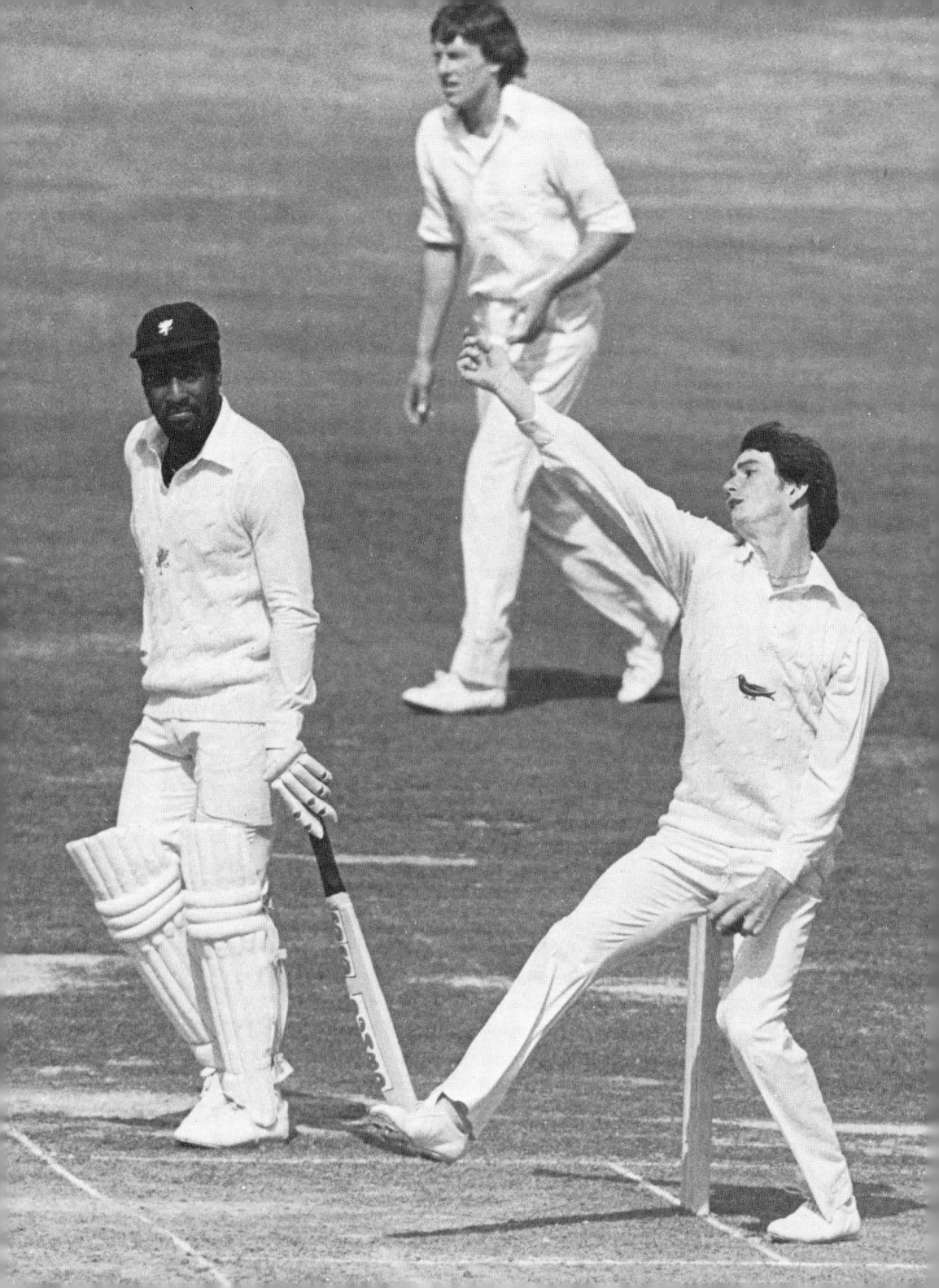

runs an over, and eventually Richards's patience broke and he was out trying to sweep another spinner, John Barclay. Now that was an example of everything good in spin bowling. Cheatle bowled to a plan, pushing the ball at Richards's legs, and giving him no room to force it away.

On days like that, when you are bowling well and things are going right, being a spinner is the most marvellous feeling in the world. You are walking on air, and you start to think that the opposing captain could send all the batsmen back to the crease, and you would get them out all over again.

Days like that are great – but they don't start to happen without a lot of hard work. So let's start looking at how you can develop your bowling to reach that sort of pinnacle . . .

OPPOSITE *Giles Cheatle and Viv Richards during the 1978 Gillette Cup final at Lord's. Cheatle's success in containing Richards' stroke play was a significant feature in Sussex's win – and showed the value of spin bowling.*

1 The Basics

For an aspiring young slow bowler only one thing matters – spin. It sounds obvious, I know, that if you want to be a spin bowler you have to be able to spin the ball – certainly it is the first thing I look for in a youngster. Yet so many coaches seem to forget that that is the main priority. If, when you are playing for your school or club, you find that you can spin the ball, make it turn and jump, you have got what it takes. And if your coach wants to make you forget the spin while you learn to develop a good length and line I believe he has got it wrong.

Now I don't mean that bowling a good line and a tidy length doesn't matter, because on good wickets it is vital. But you must learn to get the ball fizzing through the air first. Many coaches make the mistake of teaching a length and a line before they teach spin, but I believe that you should concentrate on finding the length and line only after you are spinning the ball as much as you can. If you do it the other way round you will lose the direction when you try to spin it, and so will have to start all over again, working to get the length right. If your coach forgets that spinning is the most important part of the game he won't help you.

I must admit that I don't agree with many of the coaches in cricket. They do far too much theorizing, and that can just be confusing. Too often they want to turn a promising youngster into a textbook player, instead of using the textbook to help solve problems.

12

I have seen a lot of young bowlers come onto the county cricket scene, and then disappear – and I am sure that many of them were the victims of bad coaching. In the early Sixties, Surrey produced a very promising young left-arm bowler called Roger Harman. He took 136 wickets in 1964, and looked a great prospect. But then it seemed that his head was filled with theories from the coaching manuals, and within a few years he had disappeared. I am sure it was because he was over-coached.

Johnny Wardle, Yorkshire's most successful spinner throughout the 1950s, was almost another example. Johnny was a left-arm bowler with what was, in many ways, a perfect action. He got beautifully sideways-on, using his body to put extra spin on the ball, and took a lot of wickets in his first few years. But Bill Bowes, the Yorkshire coach, wasn't happy with that. He saw that Johnny began to deliver the ball with his left hand in the small of his back. So one winter he took Johnny into the nets, and worked on trying to change his action. His aim was to make Wardle bring both hands up to near his chin, from where most spin bowlers start their delivery.

Next season, Johnny couldn't get in the side; he had a dreadful year. Luckily he had the sense to go back to the nets the next winter, and practise his old action. The results speak for themselves. He went on to take 102 Test match wickets, and to take 100 county wickets in a season ten times. But if he hadn't had the sense to go back and work on his old action, and forget the coaching, he might never have played cricket again.

Now I don't want you to read this and go off and ignore your school or club coach completely, because you must always be prepared to listen to what people tell you, and learn from them. But what you must remember is that spin is everything, and the refinements of what your bowling action looks like come second. Once you have learnt to spin the ball, then hard work, practice, bowling and bowling and bowling will make you a good spinner. But you must learn to spin it first. It should become so ingrained, so natural, that you end up finding it harder to bowl a straight ball without spin than to spin the ball.

I was lucky because I had a natural 'textbook' action. The coach would invite people up to watch me in the nets, and say: 'That is how to bowl.' But I don't think there is such a thing as a perfect action for everyone. It depends on your height, size and natural instincts.

A spin bowler needs a few basics – good finger spin, getting sideways-on in the delivery stride, keeping the left leg braced, and bringing the bowling arm across the body to follow through. If you have those, a coach's job is to give you helpful advice and make you work hard. And that is another basic requirement, a willingness to spend a lot of time practising, because there is no other way you will ever be a good spinner. There are no short cuts. While a fast bowler can sometimes have natural pace that takes him straight into the front ranks, the spinner takes longer to learn his craft.

Just look at the average ages of fast bowlers when they first make the grade compared to spinners. While the quickies are coming through in their early twenties the spinners develop much later – and that is because the apprenticeship is longer. You have to realize that you are learning, and watch what others do, listen to what you are told, and work and work at it.

I started playing cricket in the Bradford League with Farsley. I was only fourteen when I joined, and was in the first team the following season. It was a hard school to learn in. Most sides had four professionals, who were all former county players or youngsters on the fringes of the county sides. By the time I finished my National Service I was starting to play regularly for Yorkshire, and in 1953 I hardly missed a game.

The following year was very different. Bob Appleyard

and Brian Close both returned from long spells out through illness and injury – and that meant there were three of us pushing for one place, and I spent much of 1954 on the sidelines.

Now in many ways I think that was one of my most important seasons. It was hellishly difficult, because when I did get in the team I only bowled on good wickets after everyone else had failed and the batsmen were well set. But it taught me that things weren't going to be easy, and that if I wanted to win back my place I would have to work for it. Every morning I went out to the nets, found somebody to bowl at, and then practised hard. If I hadn't done that I could so easily have lost confidence, and that could have been the last cricket ever saw of me.

Confidence is vital for a spinner. You have to be prepared to take a batsman on, to keep the ball pushed up to him. If you stop believing in your own ability you are finished. I think many captains and coaches don't fully understand how nerves can ruin a bowler, but self-confidence is probably more important for him than for a batsman. A bowler gets anxious – I certainly did during that time – and he needs the right sort of encouragement to keep trying.

I was fortunate that the Yorkshire coaches Bill Bowes and Arthur Booth*helped me considerably. Arthur was a special help, because he didn't over-coach. He would just tell me what he would do in particular circumstances and then leave me to make up my own mind. And he knew what he was talking about. He was a very fine left-arm bowler, and would have been a great Test player if he had not had the

---

*Arthur experienced one of the most curious of all cricket careers. He played only twice for Yorkshire in 1931 and played no more for the county during Hedley's reign. Then after the war in which Hedley was killed, Arthur, at the age of forty-three, took 84 wickets at 11.90 for Yorkshire in 1946 and was capped. The following season his first-class career drew to a close as he was troubled by arthritis.

15

misfortune to compete with the brilliant Hedley Verity for a place in the pre-war England team.

Arthur taught me a great deal, and passed on all his years of experience. We spent hours working to improve my length and direction – but without ever forgetting the amount I spun the ball. By the end of 1955 I was getting my reward for the hard graft we put in together in the nets, and was starting to bowl regularly for Yorkshire again.

So, to gain rewards, you must be prepared to put a lot of effort into improving your game. If you can't find anybody to bowl to, peg out a sheet of newspaper where a good-length ball should be landing, and then bowl at it. You will find that your length starts to be automatic.

But whenever you can, you should try to find a batsman to bowl at. Bowling to someone in the nets, instead of just bowling, will add that vital extra edge to your practice sessions. This is terribly important, because when you are out in the middle the spot where a good-length ball should pitch will vary enormously. A perfect length to one batsman will be a full toss to another, depending on how tall he is and how he uses his feet.

I always used to hate playing against Lancashire if Clive Lloyd and Harry Pilling were batting together for this very reason. Clive, a beautiful front-foot player, and a towering six feet three inches, seemed to reach almost to the middle of the wicket when he was on the attack, so to keep the ball to a good length you had to drop it very short. At the other end Harry Pilling was the complete opposite. He is barely five feet tall, and plays almost every shot off the back foot – so to him you had to push the ball up a long way all the time. You couldn't hope to settle on one spot, because a good length for one would probably be two yards away from a good length to the other.

This is where practice in the nets with a batsman will teach you to be adaptable, and vary the length you bowl to take account of who you are bowling to. So rule one of net

OPPOSITE *The long and the short of it! Clive Lloyd towers over Harry Pilling during a Lancashire match – and illustrates the problems which bowling to different batsmen can mean in finding the right length*

16

practice is to take a batsman with you whenever you can. Rule two, which is probably more important, is to concentrate on what you are doing.

I remember in my early days as captain of Leicestershire going to watch some of the youngsters in the nets – and what I saw made me furious. They were just running up and bowling without a thought in their heads, not caring where the ball went. I watched one of them bowl six balls, with four of them going down the leg side, before I stopped him and gave him a rocket. What I wanted him to realize was that out on the pitch he could have cost his side 20 runs. I think it is vital to concentrate when you are practising. You must work at it as hard as you would if you were bowling in a Test match at Lord's.

When you get to the nets, have a plan in mind of what you will work on. If you don't do that you will bowl badly, and that means you will be practising faults. The big problem with nets is that you can make mistakes and not be punished for them – and when you are out on a cricket field you can't afford to err. You have to take advantage of nets to try things out, but you mustn't let it make you complacent about what happens.

It is no use having a two-hour net session if you are not thinking about what you are doing. It is better to devote thirty hard minutes, working at it, saying to yourself: 'I am going to bowl a length, a line, I'm going to spin it and concentrate.' If you do that it will be enough. Don't go on for another hour practising faults which will become so ingrained that you won't get rid of them.

I was lucky in this respect because in my early days the Yorkshire nets were taken by Arthur Mitchell. He was a very hard man, and he made net practice in Yorkshire like playing in a Test match. If he saw you bowl a bad ball he was down on you like a ton of bricks. Even when I was still playing in the Bradford League with Farsley we had very good practice sessions. Often we used to put money on the stumps, which gave both bowler and batsman a little extra incentive.

Not all counties have such well-organized sessions – and I'm certain that the great majority of clubs don't. I would definitely recommend that when each batsman goes into the nets he puts a 5p piece on each stump, or that bowler and batsman find the coins between them. If the batsman remains unbeaten he keeps the cash, and the bowler collects any that he knocks off the stumps. It's surprising that, however wealthy or poor you are, it makes you work much harder.

As I said, it is important to take nets seriously, and I loved to practise with Geoff Boycott for this very reason. He would play each ball on its merits as seriously as he would in a Test match. Before starting he asked where the fielders

Geoff Boycott in the nets at Karachi during the 1977-78 England tour. He sets a perfect example of the sort of concentration required to practise properly

were, and then played the shots according to the positions of the imaginary fieldsmen. Practice, with that sort of discipline, makes perfect.

Self-discipline is important to any sportsman, but particularly to a spin bowler, who has so much to learn. Discipline yourself by keeping fit, practising hard, and watching as much cricket as you can. Even now, after nearly thirty years in the game, I watch almost every ball that is bowled during a day's cricket. And if I find any of my young players ignoring the match and reading in the dressing room they get told, in no uncertain terms, to get out and look at the game.

2 The Off-Spinner

An off-spinner's success lies between his first and second fingers. That is where the energy comes from to make the ball turn. To prove that, think of Lance Gibbs. His action was a coach's nightmare – he didn't use his body, and delivered the ball chest-on. Yet Lance took more Test wickets than any bowler in history. He captured 312 Test match victims because he had tremendously long, supple fingers. He could spin the ball so much with them that he didn't need any more help.

To bowl off-breaks you have to use your fingers as levers – and if you did any science at school you'll know that the longer a lever is, the better it works. For someone like Lance, whose fingers seemed three feet long at times, that was the key to cricketing success.

Now before you look down at the stubby little fingers on your own hand, and give up trying to be an off-spinner, let me tell you that you don't need to be like Lance to spin the ball. My own fingers are not particularly long, but I have taken more than two thousand wickets in twenty-eight years of bowling off-breaks in first-class cricket.

The secret is to adapt the lessons of Lance's long levers to your own hands. Take a cricket ball, and grip it between your first and second fingers just as you would to bowl an off-spinner. Start with the ball fairly close to the palm of your hand, and then flip it out into the air. Now put it as near to the end of your fingers as you can, and spin the ball

OVERLEAF AND PAGE 24
Lance Gibbs is the most successful bowler in Test-match history – yet his action is a nightmare. He approaches chest-on, and although he gets his arm high, and his left leg is braced, his bowling arm follows through down the side of his body instead of across it

21

out again. You will find that the nearer to the ends of the fingers you hold the ball the more spin you can get.

So when you are bowling remember that your fingers are the levers which make spin possible, and that a lever must be long to be effective. You should be touching the ball only with those two fingers, and the thumb should be resting on it as a balance, not actually gripping it. Aim to hold the ball firmly enough to spin it properly, but don't let your hand get tense and grip too tightly. Keeping the fingers relaxed and supple lets them do their job far more effectively. It is important to be calm and relaxed while you are bowling, and you can help yourself stay in this mood by not gripping the ball too tightly.

The only way you will develop your ability to finger-spin the ball is by practice. Perhaps, while you are sitting waiting to bat, you can spend the time flipping a ball into the air, or wedge it between your first and second fingers to see how long you can hold it there. That will stretch the joints, and make your fingers more supple – almost like oiling the spinning levers.

The fingers are the most important part of an off-spinner's armoury – but they are by no means the only weapons he has to make the ball turn and beat the bat. Gibbs was lucky because he played in a good side, and followed fast strike bowlers into the attack. You can't take that fantastic record away from him, but I honestly believe that he did a great deal wrong. He was never too successful on English wickets, and I am sure that with a better action he would have been. He didn't use his body to help him spin the ball.

When I bowl, the studs on my front foot cut a circle in the turf. That is because I twist my body to gain extra spin. If you have not got enormous fingers like Lance, you need to gain the extra spin from other sources, and this is one of the ways. If your front foot is not twisting when it hits the ground, it means you are not spinning the ball as much as

25

you could – and remember that the amount of spin you put on the ball is the crucial factor when it comes to taking wickets.

Your bowling action breaks down into three parts, the run-up, the delivery, and the follow-through, and you have to get them all right.

The run-up is not so important for a spinner as for a fast bowler. A quickie uses his run to generate pace, whereas you need it only to help put rhythm into your action. What you are aiming for is to develop enough momentum to bowl the ball without straining, and to put in the quicker ball when you want to.

A good, smooth run-up means you will reach the crease relaxed, and concentrating only on the length you are going to bowl at. From the moment you begin your approach you must be looking down the wicket at the batsman, and not worrying about where your feet are landing. Get this right – and the only way to do it is, once more, through hard work – and you will take less out of yourself, and find it easier to bowl a long spell. For an example, watch someone like Phil Edmonds, whose run is superbly relaxed.

If you start to have trouble with your run, get somebody to watch you in practice. Ask them particularly to see whether you are keeping your head still. That is very important, because if you start moving the head from side to side it will throw you completely off-balance.

My own run has always been about six yards long – I take four paces and a jump to measure it. I am sure I could bowl off two or three yards less, but I have found that the longer run is better for me, and I've stuck to it. It gives me enough pace to bowl a quicker ball if I want to without visibly straining, and so it gives me a reasonably easy action, which is what you should be aiming for.

As you move into the delivery stride, the most important points are to be watching the batsman, and to get sideways-on. A lot of people say it is important to get the arm high as it comes over, but I don't think this is quite so vital, although if you can it gives you an added advantage. In fact, there have probably been very few finger-spinners who have got their arm right up high. Most drop six to nine inches away from the vertical, and as a rule I don't think it is possible for a genuine spinner of the ball to get his bowling arm straight up. The only person I can think of who did was Lance Gibbs, and as I have said his success depended entirely on his exceptionally long, supple fingers.

The delivery stride itself should not be too long. If your back foot drops on the return crease, the front foot should be just behind the popping crease. If you allow the stride to get too long you lose balance and height.

Much more important is to get your angle of approach right, because it balances you ready to give the ball every last ounce of spin. As you reach the crease your left foot should be at least six inches nearer to the stumps than your right, so that you are sideways-on to the batsman, looking down the wicket at him over your left shoulder.

John Emburey of Middlesex is a perfect example of how to position your feet. He gets just the right angle, and that enables him to bowl the orthodox off-spinner, and also to beat the bat on the other side by drifting a straight ball to the slips. For an off-spinner that is a very effective ball – the equivalent almost of a leg-spinner's googly – but to bowl it you have to get your feet into the right position in the delivery stride.

I said that Lance Gibbs could spin the ball a terrific amount – but what he couldn't do was make it run straight to the slips, and that was because he didn't get his body into the right position. As you deliver the ball, the left leg must be taking all your weight, and it must be braced. Don't allow the knee to bend. The whole action finishes with your bowling arm following through across the body. That makes you swivel on the front foot and, in turn, puts the maximum possible spin on the ball.

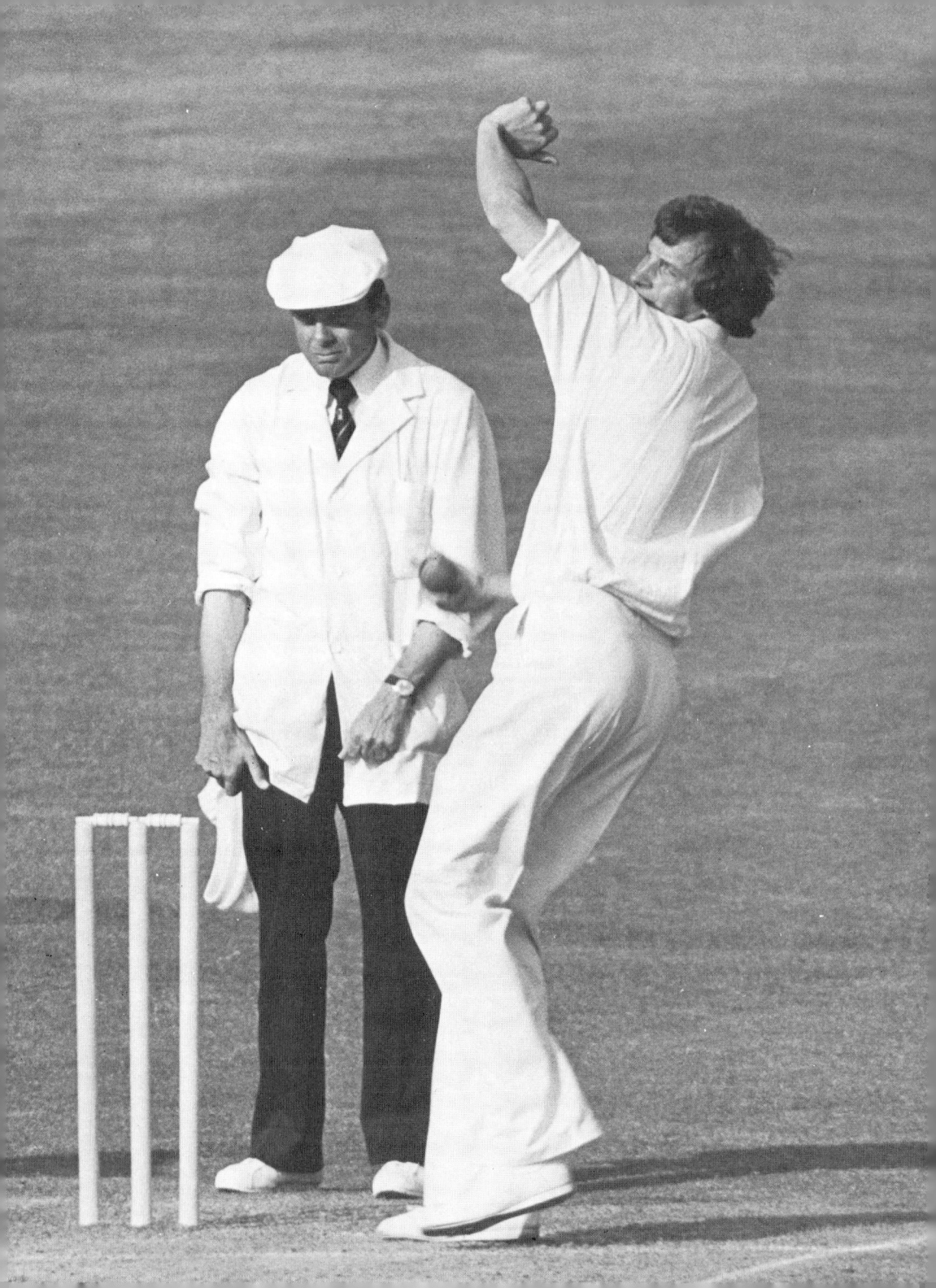

To get this right it can help to have a little slope on your run-up. I have always come in from a slight angle, because I find it helps me to get into a good position, with my left foot well across, and closer to the stumps.

Mastering all these basics of off-spinning will make you an asset to your side, because you can fill a double role. On days when the wicket is turning you are an attacking wicket-taker, and when the pitch is playing well then you can defend, bowling long, economical spells and keeping the run rate down.

The people who will support you are your fielders, and it is vital to have a clear picture in your mind of where you want them to be. I don't think it is a good idea for a young bowler to crowd people around the bat when he first comes on. You will probably need an over or two to settle down and find your length, so by keeping a more defensive field at first you help yourself. If you cluster everybody in close catching positions, and then get thumped for a couple of fours in your first over, you can lose confidence. So keep people back at first, try to bowl a couple of maidens, and you can then go on to the attack.

It is possible that you will occasionally miss the early wicket by this policy, but I think it is better in the long term, and more likely to guide you gently into a sustained spell of accurate bowling. Once you have become a good bowler then it is less important, because you will get on to a length straight away, and will expect to beat the batsman before he has had time to look at you.

On a good wicket I normally start bowling with a slip and leg slip, the wicket-keeper and myself making four attacking fielders. I would set my remaining fieldsmen according to the batsman's strengths. For a good off-side player I would have a short third man just behind square, a cover roughly level with the middle of the wicket, one man a bit straighter, and then a deep mid-off, with a mid-on, mid-wicket and a man backward of square for the sweep as

29

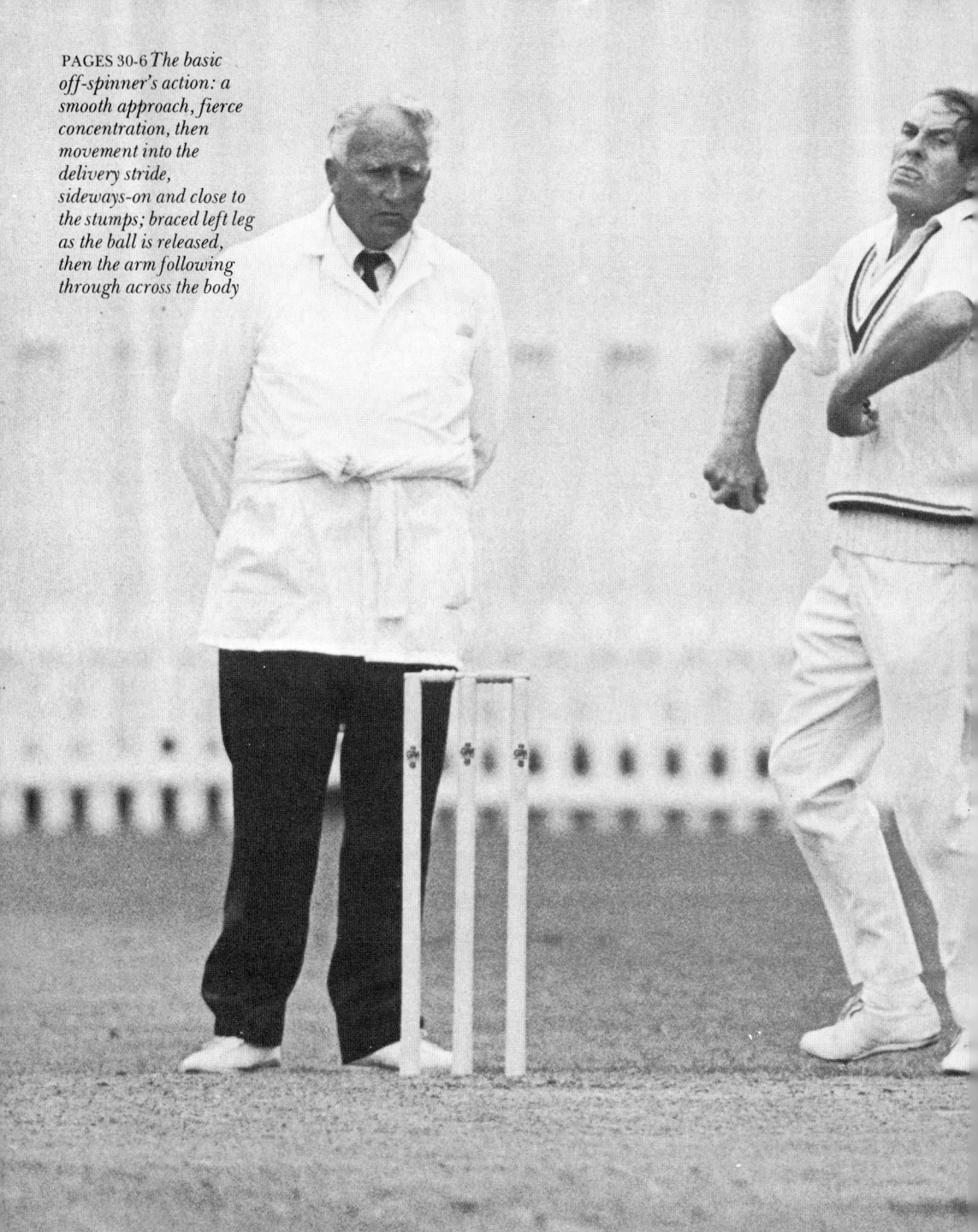

PAGES 30-6 *The basic off-spinner's action: a smooth approach, fierce concentration, then movement into the delivery stride, sideways-on and close to the stumps; braced left leg as the ball is released, then the arm following through across the body*

my on-side fielders. If he plays more shots to leg, then I would take one of the men in the covers and move him into the mid-wicket area.

If you then get a wicket or two, and you want to go on to the attack, your cover and mid-wicket can go in and become a silly mid-off and silly mid-on. It is always worth bringing them in for a new batsman in any case, because it puts on the pressure. You are loosened up and, after taking a wicket, are psychologically on top. He is not seeing the ball properly yet, and the more pressure you put on, the more chance you have of capturing him cheaply.

If the wicket is taking turn get on the attack as soon as you can. Because you are turning the ball to leg you need more fielders on that side. You could even take the slip out, and have only a short third man, mid-off and cover on the off-side. That gives you two short legs and a silly mid-on to attack with, keeping deep mid-on, mid-wicket and sweep man in defence. And if you really start to look dangerous, bring the short third man in to slip.

For an off-spinner there is no sight finer than a batsman pushing nervously down the wicket, surrounded by a ring of eager fielders. Get the basics of your action right, learn to spin the ball, and on days like that you'll be almost unplayable.

3 The Left-Armer

No modern county side can afford to be without a left-arm finger-spinner. Even on a wet, turning wicket, you cannot always guarantee to bowl your opponents out without one.

Over the years I have played cricket there have always been more off-spinners than left-armers, but that balance will soon be changed. The single most important reason for the increased number of left-arm bowlers is the enormous improvements in the techniques of pad play. By turning the ball towards the slips, rather than towards the batsman, the left-armer stops batsmen using their pads. There will be days when an off-spinner gets nothing, and the left-armer is the match-winner, simply because of this basic difference in the direction they turn the ball.

The first Test match between England and New Zealand in 1969 at Lord's was a case in point. On an average wicket Derek Underwood and I each took four wickets in the first innings.

By the time the Kiwis went in to bat a second time, the pitch had gained a rough surface, and was hard with a bit of bounce. Perfect conditions for the spinner, in fact. I bowled 18 overs, and didn't take a single wicket. I had the batsmen in trouble all the time, and stopped them scoring runs, but I could not get anyone out. Derek, at the other end, took 7 wickets for 32 in 31 overs. The different direction of his spin gave him the extra penetration.

Turning the ball away from the batsman gives the

PAGES 39-42 Derek Underwood's action is so smooth it is like clockwork. After a good relaxed approach, he is looking over his shoulder as he goes into the delivery stride, his right leg is braced and the last photograph shows that his follow-through, across his body, is quite perfect

38

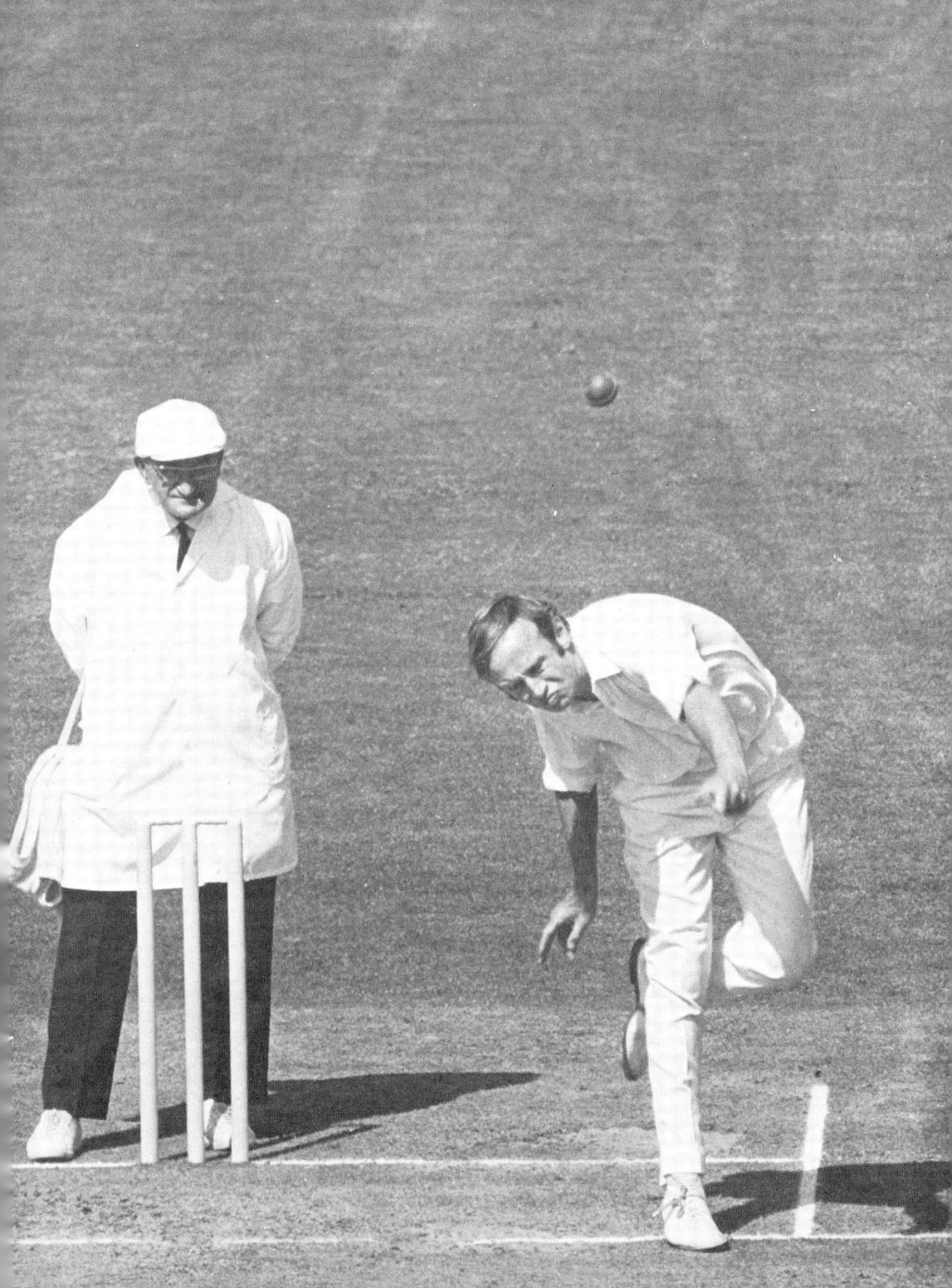

left-armer a second big advantage over the off-spinner.

If you ask a child to pick up a bat and hit a ball, he will naturally swing towards the leg-side. If you remember the times you hit the ball into the neighbour's garden when you were a kid, you'll find that most times it was the leg-side fence you were clambering over to get it back.

The left-arm bowler takes advantage of this natural swing. Against an off-spinner the right-handed batsman who swings to leg can often get away with a mistimed shot. He will probably hit the ball to square leg rather than mid-on, but he will still hit it hard. Even if he holes out at deep square leg he is still giving a difficult catch. But if he tries to play to leg when the ball is turning away, it will take the outside edge and just pop up into the air. Even though the batsman may be playing correctly to mid-off, if the ball spins more than he is expecting he will lob it into the covers.

This all goes to make the left-armer a much better defensive bowler, because he can stop people making fast runs by cutting down their margin of error so much. The influx of overseas players has changed this slightly, because many of them are strong off-side players, and tend to be able to force the ball over the covers. To do that you have to be very strong, and although people like Gloucestershire's South African Mike Procter can do it, the number of schoolboys or club cricketers you meet who can force you away like that is very small.

To play a left-arm spinner properly a batsman has to aim to put the ball through the covers, so you should always have at least four off-side fielders – short third man, cover, extra cover and mid-off. The leg-side field would be mid-on, mid-wicket and backward square leg, with the field completed by slip and leg slip. In other words, it is the field for an off-spinner bowling to a good off-side batsman.

If the ball is turning a lot, bring in one of the off-side men to gully, and take mid-wicket to a bat-pad position close in on the leg-side. The bat-pad man is a particularly useful fielder for a left-armer to have, especially when a new batsman has just come in. The line of the ball takes it from off stump towards middle and leg, and it is easy to look for too much spin and get an inside edge.

Beyond the essential difference of the direction of spin, a left-armer is an identical bowler to an off-spinner in almost every respect. He needs the same smooth, easy approach, sideways-on action and good follow-through – and bags of finger spin to take advantage of his natural turn away from the batsman.

Similarly the off-spinner can learn a few lessons from the left-armer – because at some time he will have to bowl at a left-handed batsman. Then he acquires all the advantage of turning the ball away from the bat. I would always fancy myself to get a left-hander out if the ball is turning, for the same reason that an Underwood or Edmonds would have more chance than me of taking wickets against a right-handed batsman. It gives me an escape from the frustrating pad play with which so many batsmen normally keep an off-spinner out.

The last twenty years have seen great development in the standard of pad play. If you watch a film of Jim Laker bowling the Australians out in 1956 their technique is almost laughable. Now Jim was a great bowler, but if you see those films you won't take long to realize that even the tail-enders in modern cricket now play with a better defensive technique. In fact it is reaching the stage where you can get as many people caught in the bat-pad position on the off side as you once could behind the wicket at backward short leg.

But I am also sure it will not be long before batsmen begin to master pad play against the left-armer. Clive Lloyd is already doing it in reverse, as a left-handed batsman against off-spinners. He has developed a method of playing down the line of the ball with the pad which can be quite baffling. He plays the shot about six inches outside the line

44

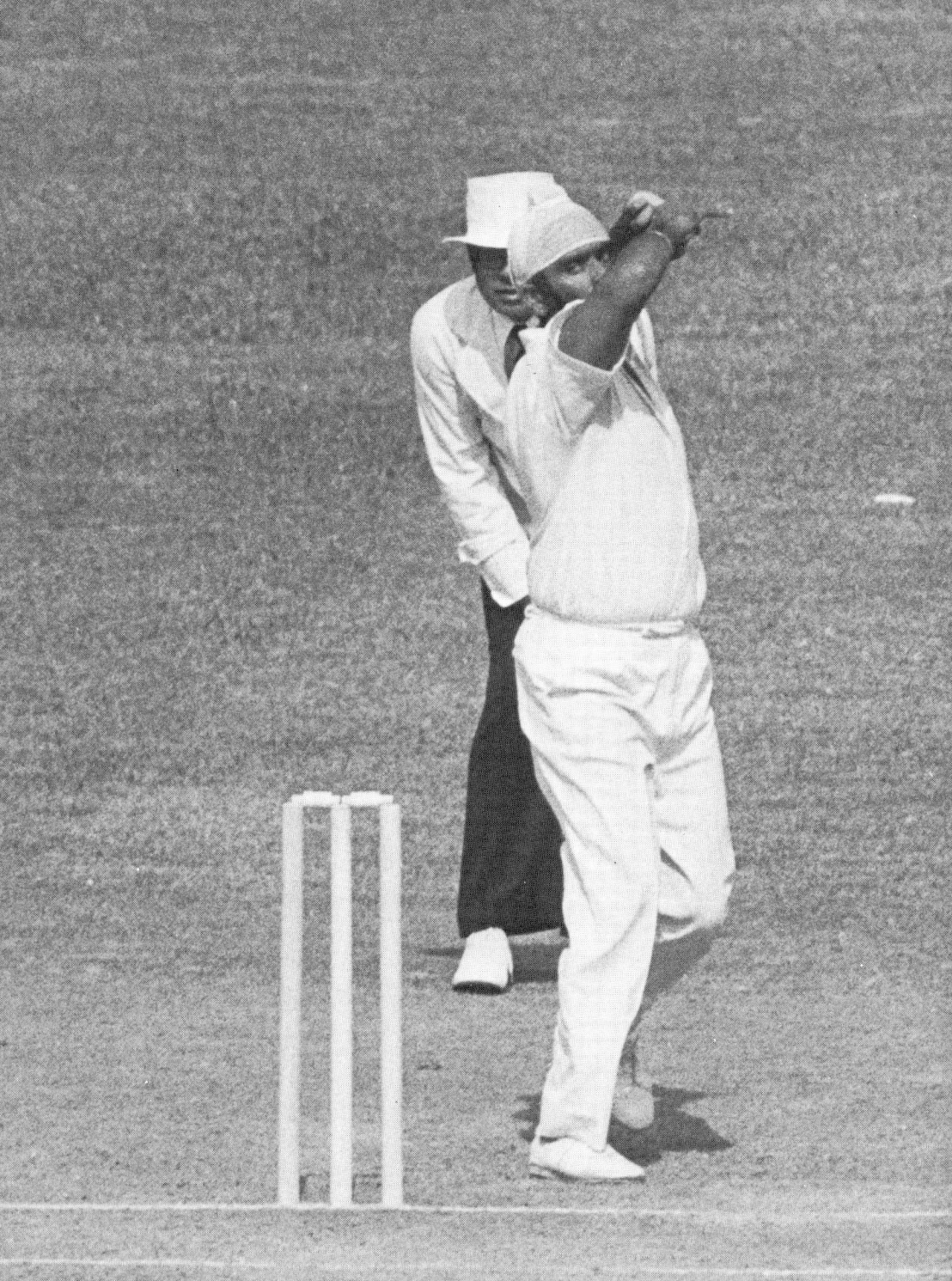

of the ball, so that if it turns he hits it, but if it straightens it hits his leg.

Bowling to Clive in my last season of county cricket I must have hit his pad four or five times in eight balls. Each time it was pitching on middle stump, and straightening to take middle, and hit his leg. But because Clive is playing forward when this happens, and is so tall, very few umpires will give him out. I have noticed one or two players copying the technique – and unless umpires do start giving lbw decisions against them I am sure the tactic will spread, and right-handed batsmen will use it to blunt the left-arm bowler's effectiveness too.

But even if the Clive Lloyd method does spread among county and Test players, it will be a long time before the average club player can master it. So for you as a left-armer, that means lots of wickets and enormous fun.

LEFT AND PAGES 50-2 *Phil Edmonds of Middlesex is another study in perfection. He achieves that vital sideways-on position from a smooth run-up, and his delivery and follow-through come out of the best coaching text books*

If you want somebody to copy there are few better than Phil Edmonds of Middlesex and England. His action has developed into a coach's dream, and would be the perfect model for a youngster to copy.

4 The Leg-Spinner

I would love to have been a leg-spinner. I am sure I would have had the temperament for it, and I know I would have enjoyed it, because it is such an attacking role.

I was brought up in an age where my job was to try and bowl the batsman out, and his job was to try to score runs. The players enjoyed it, and the crowds loved it. Now one-day cricket means it isn't necessarily the case any more, and even the County Championship has a 100-over limit on the first innings. This has made it less important to get people out; the emphasis is on containing them all the time, and that, for me, is a sad thing.

Now the leg-spinner doesn't fit into this pattern. He is always trying to bowl people out. He has to be an attacking bowler because he can't defend. I think that is the one thing that anyone who wants to take up leg-spin has to remember. He is always likely to take wickets, even when he is being hammered to all parts of the boundary.

That is why the right temperament is so vital. Bowling leg-spin is probably fifty per cent ability and fifty per cent temperament. The boy with the right attitude will always be the better bowler.

An off-spinner or a left-armer can always bowl tightly, but if you are going to be a leg-spinner you will concede a lot of runs even on the days when you are doing well. The ball will run off the edge and the splice to beat the fielders – and that is when you have to ignore the runs you are conceding and keep attacking, trying to take wickets. If someone hits you for four you must just push the ball up to him and invite him to do it again. And if he does then you have to see if he can do it a third time. If you believe in yourself and keep attacking you will probably get him, because eventually he is going to make an error.

I remember playing a Test match against India at Old Trafford in 1971 when Chandrasekhar was in his heyday. We decided to try to work him away by playing back-foot shots – and his temperament cracked. I scored a century, and the greater part of them came because Chandra lost his confidence. He was bowling short, as he sometimes tended to when he was in trouble, and by the time we had finished he had five men back on the boundary, with nobody in an attacking position.

Bhagwat Chandrasekhar's unusually fast action makes him a difficult leg-spinner to play – but I would ask questions about his temperament, the most vital asset for a leg-break bowler. Sometimes he isn't prepared to keep attacking

Now for me, as a batsman, that was marvellous, but from his point of view it was a dreadful error. He should either have kept people in attacking positions, or stopped bowling altogether. He needed a couple of people back, but I must have mishit something at some time – and if he had kept his close field I would have been out. The leg-spinner's field must always include a slip and leg slip – and on days when things are really going well you should bring in a short gully as well.

Unlike an off-spinner, you won't need many people close in front of the bat, because you won't be accurate enough. But there will be times, when you are bowling well and the batsmen are playing for a draw, when you can bring them in – and then you are more likely to profit by them, because the extra bounce you get means the ball will hit higher up the bat, and will just bob off the splice. But basically at most times a slip, leg slip and gully will be ample attackers. To a normal right-hander your field would then have three or four men in the covers, a mid-wicket, mid-on, and somebody back for the sweep.

If you do remove the attackers, so that you don't take wickets even when you bowl a good ball, there's no point in being a leg-spinner. If you can take 2 wickets for 30 in five or six overs then that is your job well done.

All the great leg-spinners seemed to have a cheery temperament – they were happy people, and I am sure this was part of their secret. So develop this. When things are going wrong look around, enjoy the view, the grass and the fresh air, and think of all the terrible places you could be. Instead you are playing cricket. So smile, run up, and give the next ball a real tweak.

And there, again, lies the secret of the leg-break bowler, the same secret that makes any slow bowler a success – spin. When you are working on your action the thing to bear in mind is that your main priority is how heavily you spin the ball. All the good leg-spinners I saw – and sadly there are very few left in the game – could give the ball a real tweak. They made it do something off the pitch.

There have been a few leg-spinners recently, such as Robin Hobbs, formerly with Essex and now Glamorgan's captain, and to some extent Intikhab Alam, the former Pakistan captain and Surrey all-rounder, who were not true leg-spinners. They bowled a bit flatter, and you could almost use each of them as a defensive bowler. Now both Robin and Inti have been useful county players, and they could keep one end sealed up tight, but they are not the sort of player I would encourage a young bowler to copy.

The sort of player I would love to discover is a good leg-spinner who gives the ball a real tweak, and will get spin and bounce out of a Test match wicket, and for somebody to do that you have to go back to Richie Benaud, the Australian captain in the 1960s. Richie was a model for anyone to copy. He got his left shoulder well round, and had a high action, and those are the two most important parts of the leg-spinner's action.

By getting the left shoulder well round, so that you are very sideways-on when you deliver the ball, you get extra spin – and with the follow-through going across the chest you can use your whole body to give the ball a vicious twist.

The high action is vital for the extra bounce it gives. Bounce is one of the leg-spinner's main weapons. He can get more bounce than a finger-spinner, which in places like Australia and the West Indies means he can get the ball to lift tremendously high – almost up to chest height on some wickets.

I vividly remember the problems Benaud's bounce caused during England's 1962-63 tour in Australia. The first Test at Brisbane was played on what was basically a dry wicket, with not much bounce for anybody else – the finger-spinners were not getting it more than stump-high. But when Richie came on to bowl his beautifully high action and sharp spin meant he was making the ball leap from waist- to

OPPOSITE *Robin Hobbs, who joined Glamorgan as captain in 1979, is one of the few surviving leg-spinners from England in county cricket. Even he tended to bowl more defensively than he should have done when with Essex*

chest-high four or five times an over. It made it terribly difficult to play, and he took 6 wickets for 115. Ted Dexter and Ken Barrington both made runs, but they really had to work for them.

The importance of bounce explains why leg-spin has become almost exclusively the weapon of the overseas player. In England the wickets are not hard enough for a bowler to get this same bounce. Even the good leg-spinners have not had the same success in this country as they have overseas, and that is basically because they can't make it rear so high. They can probably turn it more over here, but it is the bounce which provides something extra to beat the bat.

The lack of leg-spinners in modern cricket is very sad. When I started playing there were probably twenty leg-spinners in the county game. Now Robin Hobbs is the only English leg-spinner playing regular first-class cricket. It has taken a lot of interest out of the game, from both the players' and spectators' points of view. If you are trying it, then I wish you success, because English cricket is crying out for good leg-spinners.

Done well, leg-spin is a combination of all the weapons a bowler has at his disposal – fingers, wrist, body and brains all joined together to make a unit which attacks the batsman. And that is what good bowling is all about.

5 Physical Preparation

Slow bowling looks an easy life. People used to tell me that I could go on until I was sixty. 'The way you trot up,' they would say, 'you'll last for ever. You don't take anything out of yourself.' What they didn't realize is that a lot more goes into the actual delivery than meets the eye. Watch a spinner closely and you will begin to realize the stresses he is putting on his body, twisting it awkwardly as he bowls.

It is true that as a slow bowler you won't need the same type of fitness that a fast bowler does. If a quickie is going to run twenty or thirty yards, and then explode into his delivery stride, he must be exceptionally fit, and probably needs to run five or six miles every day. But don't kid yourself that spinning is going to be a soft option, because I can assure you that if you aren't fit a thirty-over spell is going to leave you very tired. To be a good spinner you must be mentally alert and able to concentrate as hard at the end of a bowling spell as at the beginning. To do that you must be fit, because you won't be able to concentrate on anything if you are exhausted.

The part of your body which will feel most strain is your back. As a spinner your action is taking you forward and twisting you sideways at the same time, and it is not a natural movement. It all adds up to a lot of stress on the back muscles, particularly in the small of the back, and this is where most bowlers tend to suffer strains. Towards the end of the day, if you are getting tired, you lose the vital ease of movement – both in bowling and in the field – and in modern one-day cricket that can prove crucial.

So while you don't need to go out on a five-mile run every day, you have got to do some sort of physical work to prepare yourself for the strain of a long stint of bowling.

The first thing I would recommend is a daily routine of stretching exercises to develop elastic muscles. I'm a firm believer in their value, and I am sure that I was able to go on playing for so long largely because I have always gone through a stretching routine every day.

The man who helped me most here was England physiotherapist Bernard Thomas. Until the MCC tour to Australia in 1970-71 I had never had any particular fitness problems. But as the battle for the Ashes went on I began to be troubled with pulled hamstrings, and I went to see Bernard about it. He explained that as you get older the muscles tend to tighten and get shorter, and that the only way to prevent it is with stretching exercises. I don't think I have had any serious hamstring problems since.

Under Bernard's influence I think all the England players now go through regular stretching routines, and slowly more county players are also starting to realize the benefits to be gained from being properly fit. These routines would certainly improve the average school or club cricketer, who hasn't got the benefit of regular exercise. There is no way you are going to keep fit sitting behind a desk or work bench all day, unless you are prepared to put in some extra effort.

The rewards you will get for going through a daily training schedule will come not only on the cricket field. You'll feel healthier, happier, and get far more out of life. That is probably enough preaching, so let's look at my own daily routine, to give you an idea of what to aim at.

I start with the simplest exercise, bending down with the legs straight and touching my toes. Doing that twenty-five times stretches and preserves the hamstrings.

The next part of the routine takes care of the thighs. Still standing up I hold each foot in turn against the buttock. I probably do twenty of these, and then the same number of groin bends, taking all my weight on one leg, and almost doing the splits stretching the other leg away.

Next come the back exercises. I have developed back trouble over the years, and these are particularly important if I am to keep it in check. For a young bowler they could prevent trouble ever starting. Lying flat on my back I touch each toe as far up the other leg as I can, which stretches the muscles in the side of the back. Then I arch my back while lying on it.

Finally, and most important of all, is the routine to build up the stomach muscles. Still lying on my back, with legs straight and feet on the floor, I bring my hands up to touch my knees. I do this exercise fifty times.

Doing this every day should be enough to keep you agile and supple. The shoulders will tend to take care of themselves through regular bowling.

Now, if the thought of fifty stomach bends, or twenty-five touch-toes, horrifies you, don't let it. Start off with much smaller numbers, and gradually build the routine up every day. You'll find you slowly increase your stamina and fitness, and feel all the better for it.

Beyond these routines you need only a certain amount of running to add to your reserves, to give you the puff to keep going for long spells. If you don't like running, well I sympathize. I have never enjoyed it. I find it boring and very hard work, and I am certain that goes for a large majority of sportsmen.

The solution I found was to develop overall stamina from playing team games, or anything with a bit of competition involved. I introduced this attitude to Leicestershire, and it was enormously successful. We had several different games we played to encourage us to work hard in training but at the same time enjoy it. The most simple was five-a-side

Physiotherapist Bernard Thomas assists the England players to limber up before a Test match. Bernard's stretching exercises helped me to keep going for so many years

soccer. I found it best when we played two-touch, which kept everybody moving all the time, with no tackling allowed to prevent injuries. It was good fun, and great general training.

Our other favourite game was a five-a-side cricket match. We had two stumps about seven yards apart, set inside a ring of five stumps. The batsman has to complete as many runs as he can while the ball goes round the circle. It was possible to score five runs in the time it took to throw the ball round the ring – but only just, and that usually led to exciting games.

These are useful routines to copy if you have nine others to train with, but obviously that isn't always possible. Another good option involves two people only. One stands with his legs apart, and the ball is rolled through them about ten yards. He must turn and race after it, throw it back, and then return to his position immediately to start again.

Another favourite is to use two balls. As the fielder turns and throws one back, the other is already on its way out to be fielded. That keeps up a constant movement.

If you have to train on your own, you can often use a wall to help. Throw the ball (a tennis ball is better because it bounces well) against the wall, run and fetch it, throw it back at the wall, field it again, and so on.

All these games involve using a ball, because I believe that makes training more enjoyable. By adding an element of skill and competition people work harder. If the training session is interesting you can get thirty per cent more than from ordinary running. There is nothing worse than boring training.

This was how I always organized the programme for Leicestershire, and we developed one of the best fielding sides in the country. That was because people were fit – and the games in training fostered team spirit. We eased up a bit when we were actually playing, sticking to a few loosening-up exercises in the morning, although during a rainy week when we weren't playing we went through a full training session every day.

In the final analysis, however, there is no better training for playing cricket than actually playing cricket. That means a long bowling spell for a bowler, or a big innings for a batsman. It is surprising that, no matter how hard you have trained, the first long innings you play will make your legs ache – just as the first thirty-over bowling stint will leave your shoulders and back crying out.

Fitness is very important, because you will never play first-class cricket for a long time, and bowl accurate long spells, unless you have good strong legs. In fact, I think almost all the people I have seen who had to retire from the game early suffered leg trouble. I have been lucky that in a long first-class cricket career I had very few problems. My legs are naturally very strong. When I was young I walked or cycled everywhere – including a two-mile walk to Yorkshire's headquarters at Headingley each day, usually undertaken with my bag on my back. I played cricket and football all the time, and it strengthened my legs.

It is now that I feel the benefit from that. Last season we played Lancashire at Old Trafford, and made them follow on. That meant six and a half hours in the field, and I bowled thirty overs straight off. Jonathan Agnew, who was playing his second match for Leicestershire that day, bowled ten overs – yet when he came off he was feeling much more tired. He was eighteen, and I was an 'old man' of forty-six, but I could take the strain more easily.

I don't want to sound like an old fuddy-duddy, but I think the reason was that Jon had not had the opportunities to build the strength in his legs because he, like most youngsters these days, travels everywhere by car. I am sure that if you think about it you will realize that you probably do very little walking. If you don't drive, you probably get a bus or train or taxi. There's nothing wrong with that, but it does make it doubly important for you to go out and exercise and build up the strength in your legs. If you have good legs you can play cricket for years. If you haven't, you won't be able to.

Ignore the people who take the mickey while you are out training hard. You will be the one who has the last laugh.

Fitness is vital if you are going to play cricket long enough to take advantage of the experience that turns you into a good spinner. That means looking after your body – both by exercise *and* wearing the right equipment.

It never ceases to amaze me when I see club cricketers wearing just a nylon shirt on a breezy day. It is one of the worst things you can do, because you will catch cold in the back so easily. This is particularly important for a spinner, because the back is the part which takes almost all the strain of bowling, so you must look after it. If you bowl for an hour and work up a real sweat, and then stand around in the field and let the breeze get at your back, you will be doing untold damage.

To counter this danger I wear a thick flannel cloth, about nine inches wide, around the small of my back, which is the most vulnerable part. Tied round my waist by two strings at the front, it absorbs sweat while I am bowling, and then keeps me warm when I come off. If there are any cold winds around it is vital.

Even with the temperatures in the sixties I still wear that, a singlet with some wool to absorb sweat, a shirt and a short-sleeved sweater. It has to be very hot for me to go without a sweater – and if it is a bit cold then I'll wear two. Watch any first-class cricket match and you'll see that most of the players follow these rules of dressing properly to keep warm. Yet club cricketers seem consistently to ignore them.

Boots are another very important item of equipment. A badly fitting pair of boots can ruin a youngster's feet. In my time they have got lighter and lighter, and I am sure this has been a factor in helping me to keep playing for so long. When I think back to some of the old boots we used to play in they must have weighed three times as much as modern ones – and carrying that extra weight all day was hard work!

Having said that, your boots must still be strong, even if they are of a more modern design. They need a decent sole, and a good heel to give support to the Achilles tendon. A lot of the shoe-type pairs don't have a heel, and they are to be avoided. The heel doesn't need to be very big – perhaps half an inch is ample – but it is vital to have one.

When choosing a new pair of boots I look for a fairly robust pair – I like to feel I have got something more than carpet slippers on my feet. Most of a spinner's work is done after the fast men have dug great holes as they pound into the crease, and I like something to support my ankles. Wicket ends are repaired better nowadays, so this is less of a problem than it used to be. At one time, following Fred Trueman on to bowl meant leaping into what seemed like a huge ditch as you were about to let the ball go.

Decent studs are also very important, although they shouldn't be too long. Their job is to hold your foot and stop it slipping, but not to prevent you from turning it. When your front foot lands it swivels round during the delivery, and if the studs are too long they will put an enormous strain on your knee, and could lead to a serious injury. I have seen people try to bowl with long spikes, and end up wrenching their knee. The studs on my boots are about half an inch long, and I change them four or five times a year to keep them at the right length.

The most important thing is to aim for boots that you find comfortable, and then always wear a clean pair of woollen socks to prevent blistering. I normally wear a thick pair of socks, and a thin pair on top, and find this prevents any real rubbing. I have never suffered from blisters myself, but I have seen people who have, and often it was

67

because they only wore one pair of thin socks – or didn't keep them clean.

As a spinner it is most important for you to look after your fingers. They are the tools of your trade. Just as a butcher keeps his knives sharp, or a bricklayer cleans his trowel, you must protect your fingers. They come in for a lot of wear and tear when they make contact with the seam of the ball each time you bowl.

The best way to look after them depends a lot on your natural skin. Mine is dry – I burn quickly in a strong sun – and I find that putting Vaseline on to keep them as moist as possible helps preserve the natural suppleness. In my early days it was common practice to harden the fingers by bathing them in surgical spirit, but I don't believe in that. The fingers tend to get too hard and split, and it can take a weak or ten days to get them right again.

If you follow my technique and try to keep the skin moist, the fingers will still split at some time, but they will heal much more quickly. If your skin is naturally very greasy then you are lucky, because you will probably be saved this problem. I don't ever remember Fred Titmus having any trouble with damage to his fingers, while myself, Johnny Wardle and Jim Laker all had problems when we bowled a lot of overs.

To make your hand stronger try squeezing a squash ball, continually trying to flatten it in the palm of your fingers. You'll find this will improve your control over the ball.

The main lesson is that providing you keep yourself fit, and look after yourself, you have got what it takes to be a good spinner. A fast bowler needs to be a natural athlete, but for a spinner it isn't so important. Going back to the 1950s, Roy Tattersall was a brilliant bowler for Lancashire and England, yet he was terribly uncoordinated, and was a liability in the field.

If you are prepared to work hard you have got all the physical qualifications you need for spinning.

6 Mental Preparation

To be a good spin bowler you must be confident. You must believe that, even if your last ball was hit out of the ground, the next one will knock the stumps over. This was one of the greatest assets of Fred Titmus, of Middlesex and England. He could play in one-day cricket, or championship matches, or a Test match with the same enthusiasm. He always wanted to bowl, to take a batsman on, and he really believed that he would take wickets – and he usually did, getting 2,812 in his career.

In contrast Jack Birkenshaw at Leicester has never been quite as successful as he should have been. One of the reasons is that he would rather have his fielders spread out than move them into attacking positions – he doesn't seem to feel he is good enough to cluster men around the bat.

It is a fact that until you convince yourself that you are on top you won't ever make a batsman think so, and this is what mental preparation is all about: backing up your technique and fitness with the right attitude. All sportsmen tend to talk a lot about luck, and blame it when things go against them, but you can make a large slice of your own fortune by believing in yourself. Watch a winning football team react when a shot hits the post – probably someone will chase on to the ball and score. Then see what happens when the bottom-of-the-table side is on the attack. As the ball rebounds their heads go down. 'That's just our luck,' they curse, nobody chases the ball, and a chance is lost.

The same principle applies to cricket. If you take wickets regularly it won't worry you that the ball is skidding to the boundary. You will already be thinking positively, deciding how to bowl the next one. And because you are willing to keep trying, to keep bowling attacking balls, you will eventually take wickets.

It doesn't matter how good a bowler you are technically. If you haven't enough confidence to exploit your talent in the middle, where it counts, then you won't get anywhere. Fred Swarbrook of Derbyshire was rated as potentially one of the best bowlers in the country when he began his career. In the nets he had everything, but when he started trying to bowl in a match he went to pieces – even bowling full tosses over the batsman's head. He did find form by the end of his first season, but for three quarters of the year it must have been a nightmare for him. This is what lack of confidence does to a bowler, and if you have never had that happen to you, it is hard to understand.

I have always believed in my own ability, and it is one of the things that kept me in the game for so long. Even when things were going wrong I was always able to bowl a length and line. Even so there have been times when the fates seemed against me, and I have gone through two or three weeks without taking a wicket, even though I have been bowling well. It is then the doubts begin to creep in.

I had a spell during the 1978 season when this happened, and I honestly began to believe that if I bowled all day I would not take a wicket. I was confident enough to keep trying, but I think it is possible that because I didn't believe I would take wickets it became more difficult. That particular run reached a head in the match against Kent, when I had two catches dropped off my bowling in the first few overs.

Then Jack Birkenshaw came on to bowl, and let a full toss slip out. The batsman swung and holed out on the square leg boundary. I couldn't believe it. I was bowling a very tidy length and line and yet he could take wickets with a full toss. As the next man came in I went to Jack and bemoaned my fate and his good fortune. He told me to try his tactics, and so the next over I purposely bowled two full tosses. Needless to say they were both dispatched to the boundary.

Yet when things are going well it is even possible to use a full toss deliberately and take a wicket, because the batsman relaxes. Brian Close took perhaps ten wickets a season like that – but you have to believe in yourself to do it.

If you expect to get the batsman out, and show it, you have a great psychological advantage. Probably the greatest man I have ever played with for this was Don Wilson, of Yorkshire and England, now the Head Coach at Lord's. He seemed to anticipate success with every ball. His arms shot up in the air, even his natural follow-through seemed to end in a leap ready to appeal. He seemed so confident that everybody who played against him felt he must be a world-beater. That, in turn, made them less sure of what they were doing, and Don was on top.

The irony was that Don was, in fact, the most nervous person who ever played first-class cricket. He would have nightmares for a fortnight about going to play at Swansea, which he knew would be a turning wicket, because the pressure would be on him to produce the goods. Yet because he seemed so sure of himself nobody ever realized.

Psychology plays a huge part in cricket. Bowling to someone means you want to test his nerves as well as his ability. Fast bowlers do that with the bouncer, which makes a batsman scared. As a spinner you must look for more subtle ways of unsettling a batsman.

A little bit of chat as a new man is taking guard is one way to do this. As the batsman digs out his mark you can tell him: 'Don't dig too deep, you won't be there long enough to use it.' Ask him how his wife and kids are, what he thought of the film on telly the night before, or tell him how well your wicket-keeper is playing. Try anything to take his mind off the task in hand. This used to go on a great deal during my time with Yorkshire, and I'm sure it unsettled a lot of batsmen. For a young player to come in, unsure of himself, and then survive the banter from close fieldsmen and bowler takes some doing.

I suppose you could argue that this is gamesmanship, but I think it is accepted as a legitimate part of top-level cricket – all part of the psychology of the game. One thing I would stress – *don't* talk while the bowler is running in, because that is unfair.

At Test match level there is always a lot of muttering going on out in the middle. It's something that people in the crowd obviously can't see or hear, but in some cases it can play as big a part in taking a wicket as a brilliant delivery.

If you could tie a microphone around Geoff Boycott's neck when he starts an innings in a big Test match, or even a county game, you'd soon learn about this. Geoff is often nervous early on, and he likes silence while he gets his eye in. So people talk to him a lot, and the more he presents a stony wall of silence, the more they chatter.

Nottinghamshire's Derek Randall is the complete opposite. His nerves make him *want* to talk – and any well prepared fielding side will always greet him with complete hush. He stands at the crease, chattering, cracking jokes, whistling, trying hard to relax – and a well-organized fielding team completely ignore him.

The Australians, who are probably the most famous 'chatterers', fell for this in the Melbourne Centenary Test, when Derek hit that marvellous 174 in the second innings. They tried to unsettle him by talking early on, and he thrived on it. When we play against him in county games there is complete silence – we really make him stew in his own juice.

Always aim to put as much pressure on a batsman as you can. Make him think you're bowling brilliantly, that the ball is turning, that he is living on borrowed time. If you can, bowl a tight length and line then push in a bat-and-pad fielder a yard from the batsman. His sheer presence is intimidating, and it can make someone play shots they wouldn't normally try in an attempt to move him.

Another thing worth remembering is that a batsman who has just got out is a great talker. He will probably return to the dressing room and describe how he has just fallen to the best ball ever bowled in cricket's history – even if it was a full toss. That prepares the new man to expect all the world's best spinners rolled into one to be bowling at him. If you can add to his suspicions you give yourself a great advantage.

One of my favourite tricks comes after I beat a batsman for the first time. The ball may not even have turned, but I still mutter to the nearest fielder (loudly enough to be heard by the batsman): 'It's turning a lot today.' That encourages the batsman to think it is turning, and if he gets out he'll go back and report how bad the wicket is. In no time you are bowling to a procession of hapless victims expecting to see every ball leap and turn two feet. On days like that a straight ball is unplayable!

I have already said how important it is to concentrate during practice sessions. During a match it is even more vital.

The man who taught me to concentrate during a bowling spell was Johnny Wardle, who was the mainstay of York-shire's bowling for many years during the 1950s. It was early in my career with Yorkshire, but it was a lesson that has stayed with me ever since. We played at Cheltenham on a wet wicket. During the first innings the ball was knocking pieces out of the wicket as it pitched. I was bowling at one end and Johnny was at the other. In the second innings the wicket had dried out, and while Johnny took 6 wickets I didn't do so well.

After the match he took me out into the middle, and

showed me the wicket. In the first innings he had bowled ball after ball on the same spot, and knocked pieces out of the wicket like a big dinner plate. That had given him a spot that took turn, to bowl at the next time round. At my end the marks ranged over about four yards and, when it had dried out, had left a reasonable batting surface.

Johnny said to me: 'That is what concentration is all about. Think what you are doing, and you can bowl as accurately as that, too.'

Our next match was on a good wicket at Edgbaston. When I was bowling Johnny came to field at mid-off, and each time I walked back to my mark he looked at me and said : 'Concentrate.' I bowled better that day than I had ever done before. On a good wicket I bowled 12 overs and took 1 for 14. Johnny came to talk to me afterwards, and said: 'That has shown what you can do if you apply yourself. I am never going to field at mid-off again – so now it is up to you.'

He didn't ever field there again, but he didn't need to. I learnt my lesson that day – and from then on, as I walked back, I always told myself to concentrate. Those two matches marked a great turning point in my career.

Another example to illustrate the importance of concentration. Pat Pocock, of Surrey, should have been England's regular off-spinner for years, but he couldn't focus his mind on the game for long spells. He seemed to want to go off and chatter to somebody every five minutes.

I remember watching him during the 1973-74 England tour to the West Indies which Mike Denness skippered. The wicket in the final test at Port of Spain was giving some help, because Tony Greig took 13 wickets in the match with his off-spinners.

Pat started his second innings spell of bowling with two or three excellent overs, and took a wicket. Then he went back to the boundary to field while Greig bowled at the other end, and he began talking to people in the crowd. When Pat

OPPOSITE *Pat Pocock in action. He lacked the ability to concentrate hard during a long spell of bowling – and that's perhaps why he didn't cure a few technical faults. In this picture his feet are facing in the wrong direction: they should be running almost parallel to the crease, rather than pointing down the wicket*

74

returned for his next over his length and line had gone – and it was simply because he wasn't concentrating enough. He ended taking 1 for 60 in 25 overs.

Bowling is just like batting. You must concentrate on every ball you bowl.

To breed this serious atmosphere before a big match I like a nice quiet dressing room. I don't want it full of people telling jokes and chattering about nothing. To me that is the worst way to start a day. I think you need to have a little bit of tension in the dressing room – it makes you concentrate one hundred per cent on the game in hand.

I don't think any player should have to rush to be ready. I like to be there an hour before the start on the first day, and about forty-five minutes early for the following days. After I have changed I go out and loosen up. Then with about twenty minutes to go I return to the dressing room, enjoy a cup of tea, and talk about the team we are playing. This is when I like to refresh everybody's memory about the tactics we are going to adopt, and finally we should all leave the dressing room to go out and play with the right approach.

You should aim to begin a game with a clear picture in your own mind of how you are going to get somebody out. Over the years I have built up a file on the strengths and weaknesses of every batsman I have played against, and I always look up the notes to decide how best to attack them. You get rewards for that sort of dedication on the days when everything goes exactly to your plan.

A good example was the final Test against the West Indies at Headingley in 1969 – one of the most exciting games I have played in. England won – but only because we had a definite scheme in mind for each batsman.

The wicket got better and better as the match went on, and the West Indies came to the last innings wanting 303 to win. At 219 for 3 they looked certain to succeed, but they reckoned without our plan. We had decided how to bowl to each of the early batsmen, and the preparation paid dividends.

It began when Basil Butcher, a strong on-side player, misjudged a ball which Derek Underwood turned away from him. I then brought Barry Knight on to bowl to the great Gary Sobers. He was inclined to be tempted into a rash early shot, and I wanted Barry to bowl a wide full length at him. The plan worked, and Sobers was bowled for a duck off an inside edge.

Then Clive Lloyd arrived, and I came on to bowl. I got one to turn away from him, and he was caught behind. Underwood returned to attack the right-handers success-fully, and we finished by taking the new ball to blast out the tail end, to win the match by 30 runs, and clinch the series.

Preparing a plan of attack won't always work that well, but it does show the value of thinking about bowling. I believe that every bowler, and the spin bowler especially, should form a definite scheme in his mind to try to capture a batsman's wicket. It is even possible to do this in school or club matches when you have never seen your opponent play before. There are give-away signs that tell you his strong and weak points.

When I have taken a wicket my eyes immediately go to the next man in. I watch him walk out, take guard, and play the first two or three balls. I look at how he holds his bat. I can soon answer a lot of questions. Does he look big and strong, likely to be a hitter? Is he going to get across to a ball on the off stump? What are his favourite shots?

If he holds the bat up near the top of the handle he is probably an attacking player, who likes to get on the front foot and drive the ball. If he holds it lower down then the cut and pull are probably his favourite shots. If his bottom hand is very much underneath the bat, round towards the front, then he will almost certainly be strong off his back foot, but not hit so cleanly through the covers.

It will take a year or so to pick this up, but if you keep

watching where people hold the bat, and their favourite shots, it will begin to tell you a lot.

Look at the batsman's stance. If it is very open, with his chest facing down the wicket, he is probably a strong on-side player. Opening the stance in that way makes it easier to hit to leg.

If his stance is closed, with his left shoulder down the wicket, it is possible he could be a little blind around his leg stump. Then you can try bowling round the wicket to exploit this weakness. Geoff Boycott was very sideways-on at one time, and he found that it left him with a blind spot around his legs which fast bowlers were quick to exploit. He took several painful whacks on the arm before he opened up his stance.

A class batsman like Boycott alters his stance when you go round the wicket to allow for the change of angle. But most of the people you will face in school or club cricket won't, and that gives you the upper hand.

The other thing to watch is whether the batsman is playing forward or back. Many are already coming forward a fraction before you bowl, and in that case, by dropping the ball shorter, you can peg them down. Or, if you are facing a back-foot player, then keep the ball up, and make him play on his weakness. By doing this you can make a batsman frustrated, and tempt him into a rash shot.

The English county game has developed a 'bush telegraph' by which weaknesses in a particular batsman soon get known. It doesn't take long for faults in technique to be spotted, and it is great fun discussing other players, and looking for the chinks in their armour. Bowlers tend to think more deeply than batsmen, and there is always somebody who has hatched a plan for dealing with a promising youngster.

If you have taken all this in, you have the mental qualities to be a very good spinner. But there is one last crucial piece of advice. Keep cool.

It is no use having worked out a plan, concentrated hard and built up your self-confidence, if the moment someone hits you for four, or a catch gets dropped, or you don't get an lbw decision, you lose your temper. When that happens you'll forget everything you have planned.

When the batsman is slogging, you have to stay calm. If it happens to me I keep telling myself that it doesn't matter: I can make a mistake, be hit for a four or six, and I am still bowling. If a batsman makes one mistake he'll probably be out. Just relax and keep trying and that mistake will come.

7 Variations

My critics used to tell me I didn't flight the ball enough, and that I didn't add enough variety to my bowling. I am sure that batsmen could have told them otherwise.

My aim in bowling a different ball was to trick the batsman – to make him expect something other than he was actually playing. If a spectator seventy yards away could spot my different delivery, then I'm sure the batsman could, and that would defeat the object of bowling it.

When you bowl a different ball you don't want the batsman to notice the change until he is already committed to his shot, because by then it is too late. That means the grip should look the same, and the difference in the flight and length should be minimal. It's no good bowling a slower ball that is obviously slower, or a quicker ball that is obviously quicker, or a flighted ball which is obviously much higher. That gives a batsman time to adjust and play correctly. Ideally he won't discover he was facing a different delivery until he is walking back to the pavilion.

As a spinner you will rely an enormous amount on varying your pace, angle of attack, flight and turn. A fast bowler can beat the bat with sheer speed. Fred Trueman could knock the stumps out of the ground before the batsman had started to play his shot. A spinner has got to find a different way past, and you can only beat a good batsman with variety.

This is why slow bowling is a game for thinkers. You have

got to be one move ahead all the time. If the batsman expects a slower one, bowl quicker: if he is waiting for an off-spinner, make it go straight on to the slips. If, as a slow bowler, you stop thinking, then you may as well give up.

This doesn't mean that you should be trying to do something different with every ball. That is as big a fault as bowling everything the same. It puts the batsman on his guard; he knows that each time your arm comes over he has to look for something different. The aim should be to lull him into a false sense of security, make him think he knows what you are doing – and then take him by surprise with something different.

I always aimed to bowl three or four identical deliveries each over, and use the other two or three to keep him guessing. Pat Pocock tried to do something different with every ball. Instead of confusing the batsman he confused himself, and was never as successful as he should have been. If you try to vary too much it robs you of the automatic flow which your action should develop.

I had four different deliveries – and now I have stopped playing it is finally safe to give away their secrets!

My stock ball was a normal off-spinner, on a good length, which I tried to spin as much as possible.

My first alternative was a quicker ball, which I still tried to spin. On wet wickets that would sometimes turn, although not always. In any case if I didn't know whether it would, the batsman certainly didn't. On a dry wicket it would just shoot through more quickly, and sometimes beat a batsman for pace if he wasn't expecting it.

My third ball was the slower-flighted delivery. The differences between this one and the stock ball were only slight – about six inches higher in the air and pitching about two feet shorter. This is one of the most difficult balls to bowl, because disguise is all-important. The two secrets are to bring the arm over quicker, but hold the ball further into the hand so that it comes out more slowly. The speed of

Spot the difference! The two should look the same to the batsmen, but one of these is my normal off-spinner, and the other the slower ball. Look closely, and you'll see that my left leg is not so straight for the slower one, and the ball is starting to come over the top of the hand rather than underneath — and that's the most in the way of clues a batsman should have

your arm, and the extra height, make it look to the batsman like a quicker full toss. In fact, it is slower and short of a length, which leaves him playing a fraction early, and not getting to the pitch of the ball, so that his shot lifts the ball into the air.

Let the ball come out of the top of the hand, rather than through the side as it normally does. It is vital to get the length right, and once more hard work is the only answer. In the nets, peg out a sheet of newspaper on your normal length, and then aim for the ball to drop two feet shorter every time.

My fourth ball was probably my favourite different delivery. It was, in fact, a straight ball, and because it didn't turn would often get an outside edge for a catch behind, as the batsman anticipated the normal off-spinner.

The difference was that instead of the seam running across my first and second fingers, it ran round the index finger. The two were still widely split, just as they were for the off-spinner, so the batsman would not notice any difference in the grip. But I let it go without spinning it, and providing my left leg was well across, and follow-through correct, it would float away to the slips. Bowling this ball at leg stump encouraged a batsman to sweep, but because the ball was moving across and away from him, if he didn't time his shot perfectly he would get an edge.

The leg-spinner's alternatives are the top-spinner and the 'googly', the ball which looks the same but turns to leg instead of to the off. Bowling either of those to a batsman who can't spot the difference must be one of the greatest joys in cricket.

Richie Benaud perfected these deliveries better than anyone I have seen. He bowled two different types of top-spinner – one which came through a bit more quickly, and the other which leapt off the wicket like a rocket. It looked like a normal delivery, even a slower ball, and was short. As the batsman got into position to pull it to square leg, it raced through and was likely to bowl him before he could readjust the shot.

The 'googly' is equally a ball which is likely to take wickets, again because it is disguised, and so has the element of surprise. The batsman expects it to go away, and instead it shoots back at him.

The aim of all variation is to break the batsman's concentration – and you can do it in all sorts of ways. Brian Close was the best bowler of a full toss I have ever seen. He would go through three or four tight overs, pinning the batsman down with accurate deliveries on a length and line, costing hardly any runs. Then the full toss would come down, the batsman, grateful for some respite, relaxed and swung – and often, because he was relaxed, he miscued the shot.

That tactic is worth trying against a batsman who is blocking everything, playing for a draw. If you have got a fielder at deep square leg you can suddenly send down a chest-high full toss. The batsman will instinctively go to swat it away, and before he can stop himself the ball is up in the air for a chance.

Against ultra-defensive batting it is very often the bad balls which take wickets. The batsman takes chances – possibly he doesn't hit hard enough because he decides at the last moment that he shouldn't be playing aggressive shots. In these situations a spinner's ability to think about different tactics is invaluable.

The other options you have in varying your attack come from the angle of delivery. There is as much as two feet of difference between the ball bowled when you are almost touching the stumps, and the one from the edge of the crease. By going round the wicket you can change the line even more. This is something to be taken advantage of, but once more you don't want to be bowling every ball from somewhere different. Use it to help you. When bowling the straight ball that floats to the slips get as near to the stumps

as possible, because you are then moving the ball away from the batsman naturally.

Going wide won't always help, because if you are an off-spinner the turn only takes the ball to the place where the batsman is already expecting it. The only time I use a very wide angle of approach is against a good off-side player who is trying to hit through the covers. If you attack him from a wider angle he has to turn the bat more to hit you to the off, and you can sometimes bowl him through the 'gate' between bat and pad. Conversely, for a good leg-side player, get as close to the stumps as you can.

Coming round the wicket is another good weapon – and probably one that club players don't fully understand. There are basically three occasions when you want to bowl round: on a turning wicket, on a good wicket when the batsman is on top and you want to try something different, and to help you correct your action.

On a turning wicket going round is almost automatic. If the batsman is a strong off-side player stay over, but if he is using his pad to defend then it is essential to go round. It means the ball is turning back to hit the wicket, rather than miss leg stump, and is the only way you can hope to get an lbw decision in your favour.

On a good wicket you would normally only try bowling round as a last resort. If, after ten or fifteen overs, you still haven't taken a wicket it is worth changing for an over or two to create different problems for the batsman.

The third reason for bowling round is probably not something you would find in most coaching manuals – but it is a trick I have used with great success. Every now and then I seemed to have a day when I lost the natural rhythm of my action. I would be bowling over, and not spinning the ball. I wasn't getting my body into the delivery, and my action had become chest-on. Then going round the wicket forced me to get my left leg well across, and I recovered the all-important twisting of the body which gives extra spin.

87

After two or three overs going round I had regained my natural action, and started bowling over the wicket again.

When going round the wicket, keep your feet in the same positions as normal, so that the left foot is now further away from the stumps than the right, and you are still looking over your left shoulder at the batsman. This is vital, because wherever you are bowling from you must use the same action. Your spin, and your ability to make the ball drift away, both stem from that.

Try not to get too far away from the stumps. Although it is often difficult, you should aim to get as close to the wicket as possible. This is a mistake that John Emburey of Middlesex is inclined to make, and it cuts down the effectiveness of bowling round. One solution can be to ask the umpire to stand back a few yards, so that you run in between him and the stumps on your approach.

All these tactics have different effects according to the condition of the wicket, so from an early stage it is good to learn about different surfaces. On a quick wicket the flighted ball is a marvellous weapon, because the batsman has so little time to adjust. On a slower wicket he gets an extra split second to recover his composure and dig out the ball which had almost beaten him.

I learnt my cricket on wickets in Yorkshire which were basically very slow, and would offer a bit of turn. Because of that I tended to push the ball through quite quickly, and pegged batsmen down on a full length. When one did turn it would normally beat the bat.

When I began travelling to other county grounds – and particularly when I first bowled on Test match wickets – I found I was bowling too fast. By letting the ball drop a yard shorter, and making it slower, I could give it a chance to turn. After I moved to Leicestershire in 1969, where the wickets were almost always firmer and faster, bowling more slowly became my natural style.

On a wet wicket it is up to you to attack the batsman. You

must push the ball up to him, and not let him get at the bowling. You know that two or three every over will turn, and you are on top. Don't give any runs away, make him work for everything, and with you firing the ball through quickly he will find it hard. This extra pace was what made Derek Underwood so hard to bat against on a wet strip. He was attacking all the time, and gave no breathing space.

Try to learn the signs which tell you whether a pitch will take turn, and how fast it will be. It is very difficult to 'read' pitches, and people who have played cricket for years are often wrong. But I have always looked at the wicket – the amount of grass, how moist it is, or how hard – and then noted how much it turned or bounced. When I see another with the same characteristics I know roughly what to expect. It is impossible to be right all the time, but you should be able to forecast how ninety per cent of the pitches you come across will play.

Even then, what looks like a good wicket can be damp underneath. The most glaring example of that I have seen was a wicket at the Oval, during a match between Yorkshire and Surrey early in my career. Yorkshire won the toss, and batted first on what looked like a superb track. Stuart Surridge and Alec Bedser were bowling, and we scored about 40 without loss. Then Jim Laker came on for one over, purely with the intention of letting the quick men change ends. His second ball turned two feet, and went for four down the leg side – and the seamers didn't bowl again. Tony Lock joined the attack at the other end, and between them they exploited the damp underneath the wicket and we were all out for about 100.

Only experience will tell you the best way to attack different batsmen on different pitches. But the ability to cope with varied opponents and conditions is the hallmark of a good spinner.

8 Support from the Team

Cricket is a team game. It may be marvellous to be the star, to take six wickets, or to score a century, but at the end of the day the team comes first.

As a spin bowler you will quickly come to realize how much you need your team-mates. When someone holds a skier on the square leg boundary, or cuts off three certain fours before the batsmen can even cross for a single, your bowling figures look excellent. But without that help your figures of 5 for 40 could read 0 for 100.

In my early years in Test cricket I bowled with Colin Cowdrey, Ken Higgs, Colin Milburn and Tom Graveney in the covers. Now all four were great cricketers, but none had the speed that's vital to cut runs off. Replacing them with Derek Randall and David Gower would be worth three runs an over.

A good fielding side will turn an average bowler into a successful one. And no matter what shortcomings their batting or bowling might have, they will be tough to beat, and difficult to score runs against. When things are going wrong your fielders are the people who will help keep you out of deeper trouble. You may be facing a batsman who seems to rival Bradman, but if you keep the ball pitched up he has got to hit you into the vee between extra cover and mid-wicket, and you can set your field to cope with it.

It is up to you to do your share in fostering the vital team spirit that saves good sides from trouble. A winning attitude makes a side thirty per cent better. In my early days at Yorkshire we always expected to win – and on days when games were close we usually did.

It was when I first went to Leicester that I realized how important that team spirit was. Nobody there was used to winning honours, and they didn't expect to. But when I retired at the end of 1978, in ten years we had taken the County Championship, the John Player League twice and the Benson and Hedges Cup twice, and Leicestershire teams had found that spirit, and took the field expecting to come top.

Whether you are playing for school, club or in a Test match at Lord's, you must do your bit to foster that attitude. If you let your head drop because you have been hit for four, you are not only letting yourself down, but the other ten people. And if you shout angrily at someone who has dropped a catch you are equally damaging that spirit. Mind you, that's a tall order, because there is no greater test of a spinner's temperament than to see a catch put down. It is exasperating, because it means an advantage you gained has been lost – and it may be a long time before a batsman gives another opportunity.

My first Test match bowling spell in Australia taught me that. It was at Adelaide in 1963. I bowled opener Bill Lawry shortly after I came on, and then Neil Harvey came in. Almost immediately I had him dropped at slip, and then the next ball he tried to sweep, and another chance was put down at backward square leg. He went on to score a magnificent 154 – and I bowled twenty overs without taking another wicket.

These things happen, however, and you won't help the cause by losing your temper about it. I have tried never to get angry at someone for missing a catch, provided they were concentrating. If you do lose your temper you lose

Mike Brearley catches Prasanna in the third Test between India and England at Madras in 1977. Look at the field positions for Derek Underwood for a perfect example of where to place attacking men

your ability to think, and the relaxed rhythm that your bowling action needs.

If you expect fielders to help you, then you have to encourage them when things go wrong, and understand their problems as well as your own. I dropped a catch during my county debut for Yorkshire against Hampshire at Leeds in 1951, and Bob Appleyard, who was bowling, gave me a terrible time for it. I felt about two feet tall, and it left me scared to do anything for the rest of the day in case it went wrong. If he had said: 'Never mind, you tried, now hold the next one,' I'm sure I would have responded far more.

I have always tried to remember that incident when captaining sides with young players. At any level a young-ster will be nervous in his first few matches, so he needs friendly help and encouragement.

Get the team on your side and it will boost your confidence no end. When you are bowling on a wet wicket, on the attack, it is tremendous to know you can trust your fielders.

The best close fielder I ever played with was Phil Sharpe of Yorkshire and England. He had the priceless gift of concentration. He could stand at first slip all day without touching the ball, and then suddenly dive full-length to pick up a brilliant catch five minutes before close of play. He would often come off the field more exhausted than the bowlers because of the strain of concentrating so hard.

Another Yorkshireman, Brian Close, was in the same sort of class. He was the ideal man to have at short leg. Brian was tremendously brave, and wasn't scared to be hit a few times. His presence so near to the batsman put enormous pressure on. Batting in a Test match calls for steady nerves – and having a Brian Close a yard away does nothing to calm them down.

If someone in your school or club team is prepared to fill that job, then you can put your opponents under the same sort of pressure. But you must remember that you have a responsibility to him as well. If you are not accurate enough, he will be risking serious injury.

You'll learn that if you do a stint of fielding near the bat yourself. I did. It was during a Test match at Lord's, with Brian Close and myself reversing roles. He was bowling, and I was a couple of yards away from the bat at short leg. He sent down two consecutive full tosses as a ploy to look for a mistake. It didn't work, and they were both sent whistling past my head to the boundary. If either had hit me I could have been seriously hurt.

'Can't you control where you're bowling?' I asked him at the end of the over.

'They were deliberate,' he replied, astonished that I was upset.

'If you want me to stay there then those were the last,' I told him. That may sound cowardly, but if your short leg is frightened of being hit because of erratic bowling he is likely to drop catches.

The most important of your fielders is the wicket-keeper. If he is on the ball he can destroy the batsman's confidence, making him afraid to use his feet against you because he knows that if he misses the ball he'll be stumped. Good teamwork between bowler and wicket-keeper is important. He must understand what you are doing and why, and be able to read the different deliveries you bowl.

Alan Knott, the Kent and former England keeper, was the best I played with. Before a Test match he would get me to go through all the variations in my bowling. I was a difficult person to keep wicket to, because I always bowled a fairly full length which left less time to adjust to the turn, and very little margin of error. But after a thirty-minute rehearsal Alan could cope with anything – and that gave me great confidence when the match began.

Good team spirit depends on this sort of cooperation. Playing for a happy team makes you put so much extra into

England wicket-keeper Bob Taylor makes a smart stumping. Working closely with your keeper pays such dividends — and puts tremendous pressure on the batsman, who daren't try to come down the wicket to you

your game – and gives you so much more enjoyment. And when the team-mates you respect invite you to lead them back into the pavilion, triumphant after a devastating 6 for 30 spell of bowling, you'll know that all the hard work it took to become a spinner was worthwhile.

9 Spin Bowlers Assessed

The pressures of the one-day game have made it difficult for young spinners to break into top-class cricket. Bowling in different competitions, against batsmen who are trying to hit everything, and with ultra-defensive field placings, is no training for a youngster trying to learn the craft.

The effect of that shows in the ages of the players in my spin bowling 'hall of fame'. Only three of them have yet to see their thirtieth birthday. Spinners became unfashionable when the one-day game caught hold, and most counties began to rely on a seam attack. I hope that trend is going to change, and the success of people like Phil Edmonds and John Emburey will encourage a new wave of youngsters.

Meanwhile I have chosen my list (arranged alphabetically) from people I have played with or against in the past decade – and added those like Emburey and Derbyshire's Geoff Miller who are still on the threshold of real greatness. For each of them I have added their Test-match figures (up to 1 October, 1978) as a guide to their abilities. In the final analysis it is not how stylish a bowler looks that is important, but how many wickets he takes for how few runs.

INTIKHAB ALAM

Strengths

Combines a smooth approach and nice action with good temperament, and gets his wrist well into the delivery. He is remarkably accurate for a leg-spinner, and that quality allowed Pakistan to use him in a defensive role at times. His top-spinner and googly are difficult to spot, and he bowls them with some success. He adapted well to English conditions playing for Surrey, and can bowl economically on wickets which don't help him, or even in one-day cricket.

Weaknesses

Because he is so accurate, and tends to be used as a defensive bowler, he doesn't spin the ball as much as he might. I am sure that if he tried to spin it more – even if he occasionally bowled a bad ball – he would have taken more wickets at Test match level. Certainly he would have turned the ball more sharply. Very often Surrey's position has forced him not to give runs away, but I like to see a leg-spinner turn the ball on anything, and he could have done that if he wanted to.

Test Record

Tests – 52; balls – 12,178; wickets – 139 for 5,129 runs at an average of 36.89.

BISHEN BEDI

Strengths
A very fine all-round bowler, his flight and use of the quicker delivery which goes on with the arm are excellent. He learnt to bowl with such guile on wickets in India which were ideal for spinners, giving help to anyone prepared to flight the ball and spin it. His smooth run-up and nice action mean he has no problems bowling long spells – and in India that often means fifty or sixty overs straight off.

Weaknesses
In a Test match it is difficult to find fault with him, but when he played English county cricket for Northamptonshire he would not adapt. He isn't content to bowl 8 overs for 10 or 15 runs in a limited-overs match, but wants to carry on trying to buy wickets, which harms the team. I know that several players at Northampton tried to change his attitude, but I don't think they ever succeeded. Three of the four English domestic competitions are limited-overs, and you can't have an overseas star who only plays in championship matches. Bedi is a good illustration of the adage that the team and its needs come first.

Test Record
Tests – 58; balls – 19,135; wickets – 246 for 6,615 runs at an average of 26.89.

BHAGWAT CHANDRASEKHAR

Strengths

Chandra is an unusual type of leg-spinner, because he bowls so quickly. His stock ball would make a medium-pace seamer happy, and he bowls a quicker one that is a genuine bouncer. His googly is difficult to spot, and it turns a good deal and bounces high because of the extra pace. A fine attacking bowler, he is always likely to get people out on Test match wickets, and that is what the leg-spinner is paid for.

Weaknesses

Like Underwood, his speed is both his asset and his weakness. The difference is that Chandra has never been so accurate. He tends to bowl at least one ball an over short, and a good batsman knows he can always be looking to get on the back foot and score runs. Providing they watch for the one that comes through more quickly off the pitch after they have got into position to pull, batsmen know they can force him away. I would like to see him make his normal delivery spin more – it doesn't normally turn often enough, and good batsmen almost treat him as a medium-pacer who makes the occasional ball turn.

Test Record

Tests – 50, balls – 14,253; wickets – 222 for 6,270 runs at an average of 28.24.

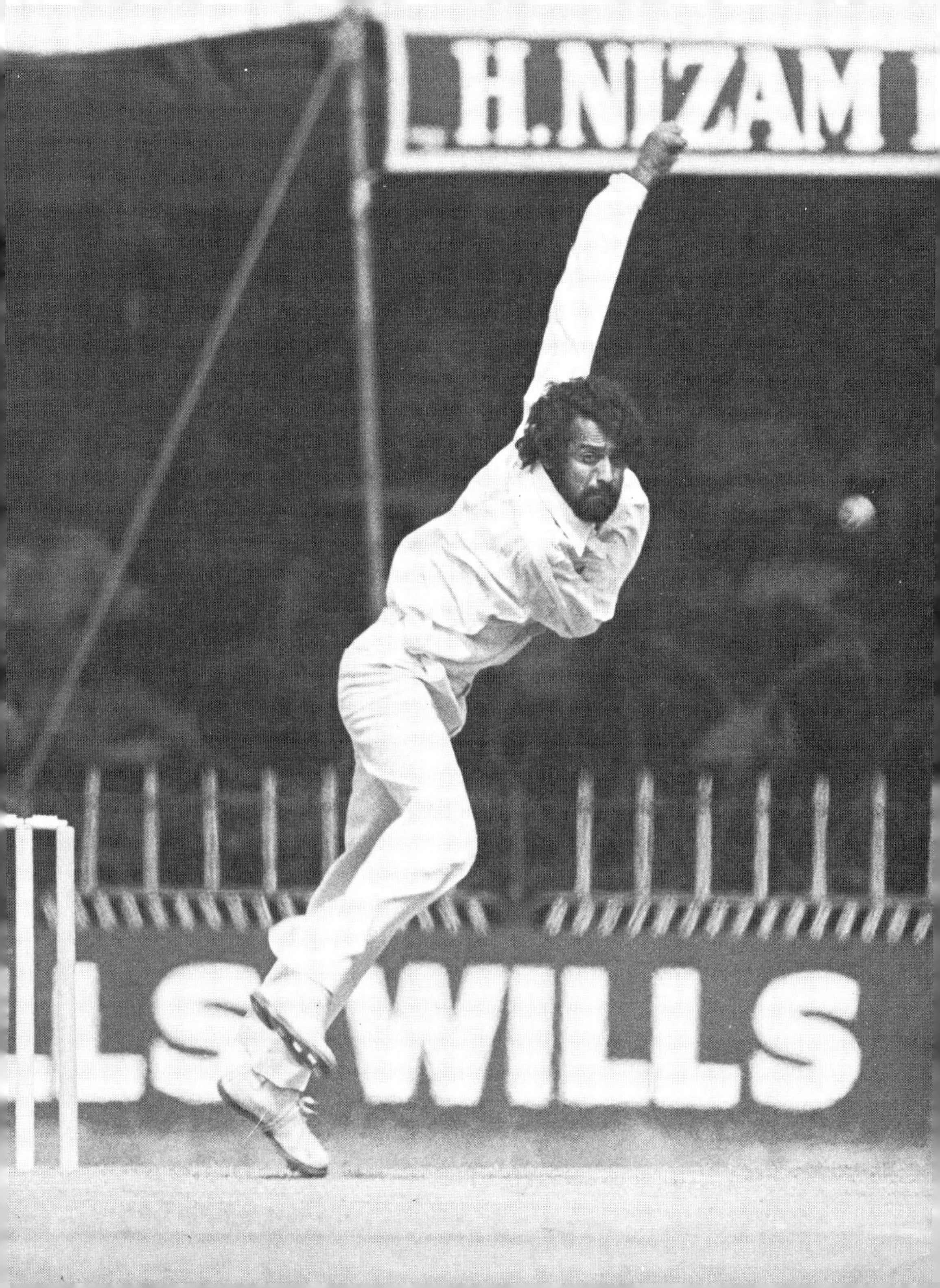
H.NIZAM
LS WILLS

PHIL EDMONDS

Strengths

Phil Edmonds, in my view, is already a better left-arm bowler at Test level than Underwood was – and that shows just how highly I rate him. There can be no greater praise. He is better equipped to deal with different types of wicket, and has started to develop the same nagging accuracy. He has a lot of natural advantages – he is tall, and has a very high action, which means he gets more bounce. I have played against him when he was making the ball leap shoulder-high, and nobody else was getting it above the stumps. He spins the ball a lot, and bowls a good quicker ball which goes on with the arm. He is a good one-day bowler, and can push it through quickly on a wet wicket. But, unlike Underwood, he can also slow down and use more flight and spin on a good strip.

Weaknesses

At one time Phil seemed reluctant to listen to advice, but he has cured himself of this to a large extent, and reaped the benefits. The 1977-78 England tour to Pakistan and New Zealand was a great turning point for him, because he began to work at his game more and listen to suggestions. Providing he doesn't return to his old over-confidence he should have no more problems.

Test Record

Tests – 13; balls – 3,013: wickets – 43 for 901 runs at an average of 20.95.

JOHN EMBUREY

Strengths

John is one of the few genuine off-spinners to make the grade in the last few years, and I believe he is going to develop into one of the all-time greats. What has impressed me most about him is his ability to beat the bat on either side – bowling both the genuine off-spinner which comes back past the inside edge, or running it on to the slips. He can do this because his body position is so good. He positions his feet well, and gets very close to the stumps. On top of that he is quite tall, which enables him to get extra bounce. His temperament is good, and he bowls particularly well in limited-overs cricket, which is vital for a young spinner nowadays.

Weaknesses

In the last year or two he has tended to drop his arm slightly, which robs him of some of the natural advantage his height gives him. I would like to see him bringing it higher – and possibly he should also aim to get closer to the wicket when he is bowling round. His exceptionally good position normally – with his left foot well across – tends to take him too wide when he is bowling round. If he can iron these points out, and I'm sure Test match experience will help, he could become an almost faultless bowler.

Test Record

Tests – 1; balls – 175; wickets – 2 for 40 runs at an average of 20.

LANCE GIBBS

Strengths

Lance took more Test match wickets than any bowler in history. His tremendously long, supple fingers meant he could spin the ball more than most other off-spinners. His control of flight was excellent, because he had to learn that art from his early days on hard wickets in the West Indies. A high arm action also stemmed from the firm pitches he learnt to bowl on, because it gave him considerable extra bounce. Like many West Indians he was very pliant, and had an ease and freedom of movement in his approach to the wicket.

He gained a lot of advantage from playing in West Indian teams with good strike bowlers, who would often have knocked over the best batsmen before Lance came on – and, of course, the West Indies produced several left-arm pace men who left him a convenient patch of rough outside the off stump for him to exploit. Even so, he had the ability to do that, as his record shows

Weaknesses

When Lance came to England he had comparatively little success in his county matches with Warwickshire. He didn't master the technique of bowling round the wicket, which is so important on English turning pitches, and lost a lot of advantage. The principal reason for his difficulties was his chest-on action. He didn't use his body to gain all-important extra spin, and couldn't bowl the ball that drifts on to the slips.

Test Record

Tests – 83; balls – 28,117; wickets – 312 for 9,296 runs, making an average of 29.79.

GEOFF MILLER

Strengths

Like Emburey, Geoff Miller is a bowler of the future. If he can adjust to the different demands of Test matches, and Test match wickets, he could achieve a great deal. He has the natural talents, positioning his feet and body correctly, and is able to beat the bat on both sides. He can get enough turn, although he isn't the biggest spinner of the ball, and his high action gives him extra bounce.

Weaknesses

Geoff probably needs another couple of years to become a complete bowler. His county figures are already impressive, but his success with Derbyshire has added to his problems at Test match level. Very often his best county performances have come on poor wickets, and he has been bowling quickly to beat the bat. Derbyshire have also used him as one of their main bowlers in one-day cricket.

Having been encouraged to fire the ball in quickly to cope with the demands of his Derbyshire appearances, he is bowling with a yard too much pace in Test matches. If he can learn to slow down, and flight the ball more, he will give it a chance to bite into the turf and turn on better surfaces.

Test Record

Tests – 14; balls – 1,736; wickets – 17 for 654 runs at an average of 38.47.

FRED TITMUS

Strengths

Fred was probably the best off-spinner of his decade. He had a beautiful easy action, and could bowl for long spells without tiring. Although not the greatest spinner of the ball, he still gave it enough to get turn in most conditions. He flighted it well, and always bowled accurately, making it very rare that he came in for any punishment. When he did get hammered his temperament was superb. He wasn't scared to take the batsman on and keep bowling a full length. His action was good, and he could beat the bat on either side.

Weaknesses

It's almost impossible to find a weakness in Fred, but if he had one it owed more to his size than his bowling ability. He was a fairly small man, and did not have the height to be devastating on a turning wicket. He could still bowl well enough to get people out, but if he had been taller he would have made the ball turn and jump a bit more, and been unplayable on a wet pitch. Height does help a spinner, because bounce sometimes causes more damage than turn.

Test Record

Tests – 53; balls – 15,124; wickets – 153 for 4,931 runs at an average of 32.22.

DEREK UNDERWOOD

Strengths

On a wet wicket Derek is the best bowler in the world – and in any conditions one of the most accurate slow bowlers of all time. His smooth run-up and action mean he can keep plugging on the same length and line for long spells, and he has done that throughout his career. His temperament is excellent. He has bowled to the world's finest batsmen, and always been prepared to pin them down and attack them.

If he was not so accurate his extra pace would have caused him problems, and he would have taken a lot of stick in Test cricket. But because his length and direction are so good his pace is his biggest asset, because it makes it impossible for a batsman to get at him – and, on a wet wicket, makes him almost unplayable.

Weaknesses

Derek's weakness is probably a result of the pace which is normally his strength. On some wickets where a more orthodox finger-spinner would get turn he doesn't, and it is mainly because he bowls too fast. I have played with him on several occasions when, if he had bowled a bit slower, and given the ball a chance to turn, he would have reaped greater rewards for his skill.

Test Record

Tests – 77; balls – 19,698; wickets – 272 for 6,883 runs at an average of 25.30.

RAY ILLINGWORTH

I've always found it difficult to stand back and observe my own strengths and weaknesses, so I'll just give my vital statistics and leave you to decide for yourself.

Test Record
Tests – 66; balls – 12,924; wickets – 133 for 4,268 runs at an average of 32.09.

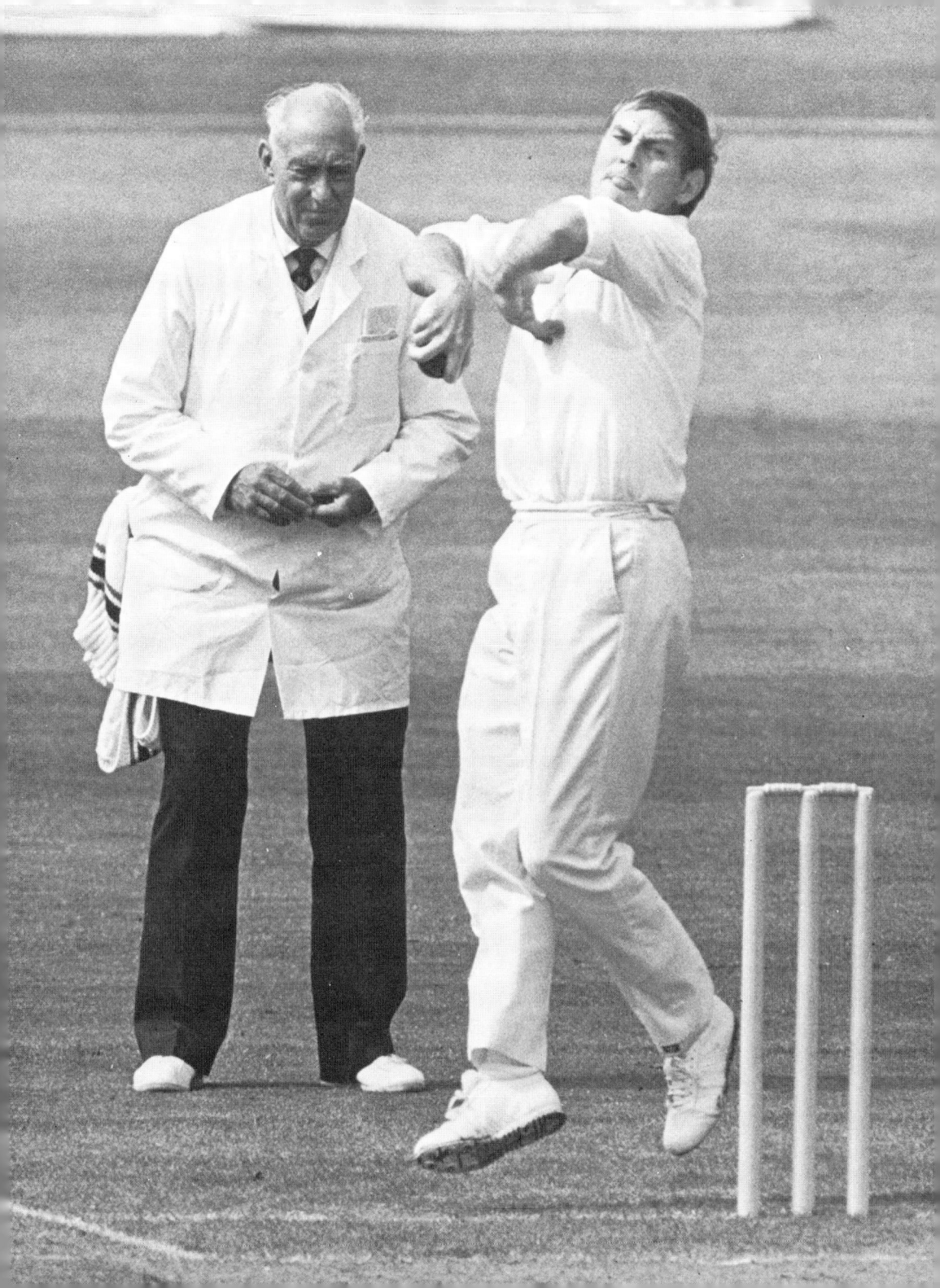